LARRY RUSHTON

A TRUE STORY

ARTIST AMONGST THIEVES

Based on the memoirs of Larry Rushton (provided on recordings Larry made prior to his death in 2006)

The names of certain individuals in this book have been changed to protect their identities.

ARTIST AMONGST THIEVES

Larry Rushton

A True Story by Derek Zimmerman

www.warcrypress.co.uk

ARTIST AMONGST THEIVES: Larry Rushton - A True Story

Author: Derek Zimmerman

ISBN: 978-1-912543-39-7

Based on the memoirs of Larry Rushton (provided on recordings Larry made prior to his death in 2006.) The names of certain individuals in this book have been changed to protect their identities. The author disclaims, as far as the law allows, any liability arising directly or indirectly from the use or misuse of any information contained in this book.

Printed and bound in Great Britain by PMM Group Ltd, UK.

Book Cover Design by Gavin Parker Art - gavinparker.uk

Find out more at facebook.com/warcrypublishing/

CHAPTERS

INTRODUCTION

This book reflects on the true life Story of Laurence Rushton (Larry as he was more commonly known) born in Burnley on the 14th May 1930. He was one of five children having sisters Anne and Mary, and brothers in Tom and John. Although he spent his early life in Burnley he always considered his real home to be on the Fylde coast, living mainly in Lytham St. Annes and Blackpool.

Larry was a person who would stand out from the crowd, a colourful character with a colourful past. His life was never dull, he lived life on the edge regardless of the consequences, he surely lived life to the full. Throughout his life there were many up's and down's, his life became a bit of a roller coaster. Over the years he endured many hard and painful times and also some very good ones.

Prior to Larry's death in 2006 at the age of 76 he had been voice recording his life story. This book is based on those recordings they cover a fascinating journey a journey full of incident which truly began in 1944 when at the tender age of just 14 Larry leaves school, not that he spent much time there he was always playing truant.

Upon leaving school circumstances dictated and Larry soon graduates into becoming a professional criminal. However, it is his criminal activities and imprisonment that reveal Larry's hidden talent, that of an artist. His portraits, oil paintings, water colours, and pastels go on to earn him national recognition as an exceptional artist.

This book features major episodes in his life:

- Teenage years
- Borstal
- National Service / Scams
- Brushes with the law
- An array of criminal activities spanning 30 years.
- The pain and hard times endured
- Robbery / Bank Robbery
- Prison life / Experiences
- Association with Ronnie Biggs
- Prison breaks (maybe fastest in UK history)
- Hitmen
- Most wanted in England
- Times on the run
- Discovering his artistic talent
- Becoming a renowned Artist / Portrait painter

CHAPTER 1

ON THE ROAD TO A LIFE OF CRIME

1944 - 1946

They say life begins at 40 well in Larry's case it truly began at 16 when he was put into Walton Prison, Liverpool for his first offence, well not his first offence but the first time he had actually been caught. He was sentenced to 3 years borstal, a sentence many people considered rather harsh at the time, but Larry having robbed pretty much everywhere in Burnley thought "Yes, maybe this sentence was justified."

Larry remembered vividly the time he was taken to a cell in Walton prison, as the cell door was slammed shut behind him reality kicked in. For the time being he would be held in what was a dirty old Victorian cell. There was bed, a chair to sit on, a small shelf fastened to the wall and a toilet pot, the only source of light was that coming from a glass panel on the wall, a type of gas light. The smell of that first night in Walton prison never left Larry, the smell of generations of unwashed people and the stench of urine. Many a time over the years when visiting older buildings that smell from his first time in prison always came flooding back to him, along with the memories of his incarceration.

How did Larry end up here at the age of just 16, well his path to a life of crime was a relatively easy one, having left school at the age of 14 Larry started work in a rope factory which was located by the side of a canal in Burnley. Larry's job was assisting in the making of rope he would walk the full length of the building time and time again backwards and forwards until the rope was all twisted and perfectly formed ready for inspection. As a junior he also remembered being given all the scrappy jobs, the ones nobody really wanted to do and he guessed this was probably down to him being the newest recruit.

Larry disliked the foreman from the minute he spoke to him, he came over as a real bully and not at all what he expected from someone of authority on his first day at work. The foreman was constantly shouting at the employees showing no signs of appreciation of the hard work that was being put in. After working all morning, it was time for a lunch break, Larry sat down with the other lads on the bales of rope looking forward to the sandwich his mother had made him, it was only bread and jam but it smelt so good he was so hungry by now the filling was of no relevance.

Just as he was about to tuck into the sandwich the foreman shouted over at him

"Get up there Rushton and bring that bleeding bobbin down."

The walk alone to do this was about 800 yards each way, it would have taken his lunch break and longer just to get it done.

Larry replied defiantly

"I am just having my lunch break like the rest of the lads"

In an instant the foreman knocked the jam sandwich from his hand. As the sandwich landed on the floor the other lads just started laughing, but Larry was in no laughing mood, he was filled with anger and without thinking twice he caught the foreman with a couple of punches. The foreman just sat down and like the bully and coward he was had no fight in him, he just screamed at Larry

"You are sacked!"

Larry was now concerned about going home and having to tell his parents he had been sacked on his first day so he decided to keep the sacking from them. His dad was a strict man, a good one, but would not have been pleased about his son being sacked, especially on his first day. Larry now had no choice but to act as if nothing had happened so each day he would take the packed lunch his mother had prepared for him and pretend to set off to work.

Having no job to go to Larry's life of crime was just beginning, more of a necessity rather than a choice of path to go down. He needed to bring home wages each week and in his mind there was only one thing he could think of… thieving.

At this time in 1944 rationing was going on, it was a really tough time for people and Larry often used to wonder how his parents coped. His two sisters were working in munitions and one brother in a shoe factory, so I guess their weekly contributions helped, but times were hard and Larry wanted to contribute as much as he could to help his parents and family out. A lot of stews were made in those days it was just a case of what you could get hold of really.

Larry can remember his dad making a big stew on a Saturday which would have to last for a few days. With Larry now thieving, food would appear from nowhere much to his mum's surprise, Larry would just say he had been given it. On one occasion Larry came home with a huge tin of corned beef which butchers used to slice up back then. His Mum grew suspicious, this wasn't the kind of thing anyone was giving away back then.

"Where has that come from Larry and don't lie to me" She said.

"I found it in town. It must have fallen off a lorry I guess, I was in the right place at the right time" He replied.

His mum didn't believe him for one minute and nor would have anyone else.

"This has been stolen hasn't it"

She continued "No mum honestly I just got lucky"

If his mum knew the corned beef had been stolen she wouldn't have taken it, absolutely not. She was a very honest lady and would have been devastated to know what her son was becoming, nicking everything in sight. This was now more than getting by, Larry was fully embroiled and his criminal exploits were about to reach new levels.

Larry through a few contacts was introduced to a local fence by the name of Mrs Pickup, she was like a female Fagin, she had been in the job so to speak for many years and would buy absolutely anything, her network of buyers was so wide there was nothing she wouldn't take. Larry visited her home regularly a real scruffy place overrun by cats. Larry's first thought was "what am I doing here" he was not keen on her at all but she was the key fence in the area even if she did exploit the many kids who worked for her. At this first meeting Mrs Pickup gave Larry a list of the items she was after, meat, cigarettes, stockings, items that were in great demand and hard to come by during what was a difficult time in life for so many people.

After that first meeting Larry contacted his pal Robert who was also always out on the rob and discussed with him the idea of taking on a butcher's shop, one Larry had been staking out for sometime. This butchers did a roaring trade the owner must have been raking it in if the car he used to drive around was anything to go by. This was an opportunity not to be missed so Larry arranged to meet Robert at the butchers later that night, no time was wasted he was to bring with him a crowbar belonging to his parents and be prepared to lump the stolen meat to Mrs Pickup's place.

The two met up later that evening, Robert was interested in how much they might get for the meat.

"Robert I don't know but let's just take as much as we can carry" said Larry.

Once inside the butchers Larry spotted the biggest piece of beef he had ever seen in his life, it looked like half a cow. It was to be hoped Mrs Pickup had butchering skills if she wanted to break it down and make the most out of it financially

"Robert we have got to take this beef I will take the beef you just grab what you are able to carry" said Larry

Larry with this huge piece of beef slung over his back and Robert with a big piece of lamb left the butchers and made their way through the back streets in darkness. When they arrived at Mrs Pickups, Larry looked like he had been shot or wounded he was covered in so much blood from top to toe.

Mrs Pickup was extremely pleased and said she would get it cut up and sold the next day. Larry asked if he could just get cleaned up a little, having done his best he then sneaked back home and crept in to wash his clothes. His family were asleep and in any case his mother never really missed him, she always seemed too wrapped up in herself and never really showed any emotion to Larry. Larry always wondered why she was like this and found out years later that she had been diagnosed with Parkinson's disease and that it wasn't personal.

The following day the pair visited Mrs Pickup to collect their spoils and received around £20 each for the meat which was a tidy sum at the time, she then asked them if they could get some more. This they did for a few weeks, they hit the same butcher using the same routine. They just couldn't understand how the butcher hadn't noticed or was just not bothered for some reason. This carried on until on one Saturday evening Larry had a bad feeling a gut instinct that this had to be the last time.

"Robert after tonight we can't do this again or we will get rumbled" said Larry.

On this occasion Larry took a look around the shop instead of just grabbing the meat, in the front part of the shop he found what looked like a cash draw, this he forced open and found £200. Jackpot! who needed Mrs Pickup he thought.

"Robert forget the meat we don't need it I have just found £200 so let's just leg it" said Larry.

Other targeted shops were sweet shops one in particular near the local swimming baths, more of a lockup really but it did a thriving business and Larry knew there had to cash tucked away in there somewhere. The pair of them emptied it one night and also looted the till. Mrs Pickup was well pleased with the sweets quite often after that you would see her sucking on a humbug or chewing a caramel, it would be doing the teeth she had left no good at all, the ones she had left. Larry also took some of the sweets home and gave them to his dad saying his friend was on a bit of a fiddle. The whole family were sick of even looking at sweets after about a week.

Larry was now the number one lad for Mrs Pickup and this enabled him to take home what was now a supposedly weekly wage on a Friday night. He would sometimes give his mum a little extra money but not too much so as not to arouse her suspicions. Larry just told her he had worked a few extra hours. His parents knew nothing of what was going on and just got on with their lives, though maybe somewhere deep down they knew that things didn't really stack up.

With Larry still Mrs Pickup's number one she introduced him to a professional criminal called 'old Mick', he was always very smartly dressed, shoes immaculate and was probably somewhere in his fifties. He cut the figure of of a local gangster, the type Larry would eventually aspire to. Old Mick had heard a lot about Larry and particularly how good he was at climbing so asked Larry if he would be interested in working for him. Larry exaggerated how good he was but was confident nothing would be a problem. The first job was to be a tailors' shop outside of town, one away from prying eyes. Old Mick drove Larry to the premises pointing out how secure the first two levels were, bolted up with bars on all of the windows. However, the upper level wasn't as secure, entry via windows was relatively easy if you could reach them.

Having surveyed the premises, the job was on. This building was higher than Larry had ever attempted before but he was very agile and eager to impress Old Mick. The thought of taking on the challenge gave him a real buzz, would he be able to make it? Larry scaled up to the 3rd floor broke in through a window and then let old Mick in the side door, which had been bolted. Old Mick knew exactly what material he was after, so the gear was loaded into his car, Larry through a few extra shirts in as well, job done.

At age 15 Larry was now making serious money, some of which he put to one side. He would now attire himself with new clothes and shoes but still had to be careful as his parents were becoming ever suspicious of how he could afford such items. With Robert living close by Larry decided to hide his new gear at Robert's, changing pre and post going out.

Now with money in their pockets the pair of them dressed up in their new gear and looking the business would hang out in local pubs and dancehalls, of which there were only two in Burnley at the time. The world was a much smaller place back then. One place they visited frequently was called the 'Weavers' it was an old church hall converted into a dancehall on Saturday nights. They were aged 15 but acting more like 17 and easily getting away with it.

Larry's lifestyle was now falling into a pattern out all week robbing and then having a good time at the weekends. Money was now no object Larry was like 'Jack the Lad' splashing the cash buying drinks for everyone. Usually women and other crooks. In those days most people walked everywhere there was no calling for a cab, on Larry's walk home he would always call in at an old pie shop for pie and peas, something that held fond memories of those days for him.

The thieving was going well but Larry had been on edge for some time wondering if he was being watched, things seemed to be running a bit too smoothly, a friend of his had been arrested for shoplifting and he then heard on the grapevine that the police may indeed be taking a good look at himself. Unsure of what is pal might say under police questioning Larry decided he needed to leave Burnley, he daren't risk hanging around. Larry didn't want to leave without telling Robert his good friend so before leaving he met up with Robert to explain the situation.

"Robert I am going to do a runner to London before the police come knocking". Said Larry

Robert thought about this for a moment or two before replying

"I am coming with you Larry if the police are looking at you they are most likely tracking my activities too". He was sure of it.

That was it the pair were going to move to London and sharpish. Larry left his mum a note

Mum,

I am not happy with my job so I am moving away to find a better one.

Please don't worry about me I will be fine.

I will see you again soon and will make sure that I send you money on a regular basis.

Love Larry

The pair of them arrived at the train station for the night train to London, without tickets of course they were not going to pay that's what everyone else had to do not them. They boarded the train which was extremely busy mostly with people in the forces heading back to camp. Larry was now feeling quite excited this was going to be an adventure like no other his first trip to the capital, surely bigger fortunes and opportunities would be found there.

Arriving in London they had no idea where to go but after asking a few people were directed to a small Bed & Breakfast. After giving false names and claiming they were 17 they agreed to pay 2 weeks up front for a discounted rate, they were sorted for now whilst familiarising themselves with the big city and put together a plan.

They walked around for 2 or 3 days, the buzz of London was both frightening and exciting especially with the bombing raids going on. Many of the streets were wrecked, buildings blown down, shops with no windows always attractive to someone in Larry's line of business but there was nothing in them they were completely empty.

Larry turned to Robert and said

"One night we will stay out all night whilst the bombing raids are going on and have a good look around" looking to exploit the situation somewhat.

This they did and ended up in the vicinity of Piccadilly in the west end, there was a lot of activity going on as bombs were being dropped, sirens where whirring, ambulances racing down the streets, people running up and down in blind panic. This made them both begin to realise more of what the world was really all about., there time in Burnley up in Lancashire had been somewhat sheltered. Still being only young they hadn't really connected with the war and what was taking place, all the suffering that was going on and that sombre feeling stayed with Larry for the rest of his life, instead of just being aware of himself he was now aware of other people, seeing people with nothing and seeing how badly hurt some of them were was a real eye opener for Larry just a young kid from Lancashire.

On one particular evening at around 11 p.m. Larry and Robert were out in the city when suddenly in front of them there was a massive flash, houses and shops collapsing, falling into each other from the air raids. The pair looked at each other and couldn't believe what had just happened right in front of their eyes, there was little noise, so they assumed it may have been a V2 rocket. As fate would have it maybe they were supposed to be there on that night at that time because shortly after they heard a dog barking next to an old lady who had been trapped by some falling doors, it must have been her dog. Larry & Robert dashed over and managed to free her from the rubble. The old lady was still in shock but didn't look badly injured Larry took his coat off and put it under her head to form a makeshift pillow and ease her injuries. By that time more people were on the scene and the dog had stopped barking, maybe it was the dog's way of saying thanks. The police had now also arrived on the scene and people were explaining how the pair of them had helped the old lady.

The police said "Will be with you shortly lads" in a seemingly thankful tone.

Whether their involvement had been honourable or not this was the indication to leave the scene and without hesitation they did a runner leaving the area before the police had a chance to speak to them. They never knew how the old lady faired, but were glad to be in the right place at the right time, if they hadn't been there she may have died or at least have been more severely injured with buildings collapsing all around her.

CHAPTER 2

LONDON / BORSTAL

1946

Larry and Robert had now been in London for only 2 weeks and cash was beginning to run out, so it was back to what they knew best… Thieving! They needed to get some money by hook or by crook or they would be sleeping on the streets within the next few days. Not wanting to take anything on too difficult they targeted shops similar to those they had targeted back in Burnley, such as bakers, stealing tills off counter tops, which were real heavy lumps, nothing like the tills these days.

The routine which they carried out about 15 times consisted of Larry entering the shop asking for a loaf of bread or other goods and then pretending to accidently drop some money over the counter. Whilst the assistant was bending down to pick up the money Larry would grab the till off the counter whilst Robert standing by the door would open it as Larry approached enabling them to make a speedy exit.

On one occasion a young man chased after them as they fled through various streets and down the alley ways. Larry being a lot fitter than Robert was well away, with Robert lagging far behind. Larry turned around to see that Robert had been caught by the young man, he put the till down and shouted "Let him go or you will regret it."

The young lad refused so Larry landed a punch on him and a fight ensued, Robert joined in head butting him. The young man now on the floor and was up for no more so the pair of them fled with the till which had enough cash in it to last them around a couple more weeks.

On another occasion the same routine was tried at a newsagent shop. However, this didn't go at all to plan, as Larry was fleeing with the till all of a sudden he was laid flat on his back, the till had a chain on it which he hadn't noticed. With customers screaming the shop assistant jumped over the counter and approached Larry who side stepped him and then gave him a left hook. The pair of them then ran away leaving the till behind, that particular incident had been a complete disaster for the pair of them and meant they'd have to take on another job of some kind and sooner rather than later. After this incident they decided they'd had enough of doing tills, it had worked and kept them going but enough was enough. The pair of them continued thieving, stealing anything they could put their hands on, if they wanted new clothes, shirts, shoes, etc. they would just steal them, they were now so good at stealing there was very little they could not put their hands on.

London was a real adventure but Robert was now becoming homesick and wished to return to Burnley to be with his family and friends. Larry wasn't sure this was a good idea as returning to Burnley would more than likely end up with him being arrested, if not immediately, not long after. Larry therefore wished Robert a safe journey and he remained in London staying in the Bed & Breakfast the two of them had shared.

Larry's instinct was right Robert was arrested shortly after returning to Burnley and with Larry's London address tucked away in his pocket it was not long before the police came knocking. Larry was duly arrested and taken back to Burnley for questioning. Statements made to the police by 'so called' friends implicated Larry. He was pretty much blamed for all the robberies, about 200 of them in total. His father couldn't believe what his son had been up to, the police had told him Larry was the worst of all those that had been charged.

Larry now just 16 years of age appeared in crown court with four of his friends where they were all given 3 year sentences in Borstal for what was deemed their 1st offence. In the scheme of around 200 robberies that notion was somewhat ridiculous. The judge in sentencing Larry warned him if he ever appeared in front of him again he would go down for a very long time. Larry's father had to work but his mother was in court to watch the sentencing and was now extremely upset, he told his mother not to worry and that he would probably enjoy Borstal, in a strange way it would be another adventure, making light of the situation.

After being sentenced Larry was taken down to the holding cells before being transferred to Walton prison, Liverpool. Life had truly started for him now. Whilst in his cell Larry soon realised prison was nothing like what he thought it would be. His clothes and belongings were taken away before he was shown the bathroom where all new inmates would wash and be disinfected. Prison rags given to him, old shirts and trousers, if they fitted they did, if not you just had to put up with badly fitting clothes, something far removed from how Larry was used to dressing. At that time in 1946 all inmates had a cell of their own with young prisoners being held in a segregated section of the prison. In the morning inmates would be let out the cells for breakfast, which would usually consist of a small bowl of porridge and a stale rock hard piece of bread. After breakfast they would be taken down to the bottom of the prison where they would sit on a chair and sew mailbags, no talking allowed. This is where Larry met up with Robert again who had clearly been crying, he wasn't taking this prison life at all well.

Robert whispered to Larry,

"I am really sick about this Larry. If I had not gone back to Burnley or at least not written your address down you may not have been arrested".

Larry whispered back

"Don't worry Robert, don't worry it's not a problem it was probably only a matter of time before I was caught anyway".

For Lunch it was a bowl of slop and vegetables, absolutely horrible stuff nothing like Larry was used to. Exercise was taken in the courtyard where they would walk around in circles still not supposed to be speaking. So the daily routine was set, breakfast, sewing mailbags, lunch, sewing mailbags and then back to your cell. A monotonous cycle of repetitive events. Both Larry and Robert were now feeling pig sick about this situation they had found themselves in as they thought they were going to spend 3 years in Walton prison doing the same routine day in day out. However, as they were young offenders they were to be moved to a more appropriate prison,

Robert looked at Larry and said "The sooner we get there the better."

Larry replied "As soon as I get there I am going to leg it." With a glint in his eye.

Robert was now only interested in doing his time and returning home. He didn't want any part of Larry's devious plans. He'd had enough of being a crook and just wanted to live a normal life.

Prior to moving to a Borstal prison the pair of them were transferred to Wormwood scrubs in London, from here they would be allocated a prison. Whilst in Wormwood Scrubs all the lads on the way to and from their cells had to walk past dining tables in a large wing which housed prisoners on long sentences, some lifers and some privileged prisoners who would sit together at night playing cards, chess or whatever happened to be available. Well these privileged prisoners used to leave a lot of bread from breakfast on the dining tables to have with their lunch, it looked as if they all had their own particular seat. One morning whilst passing these tables Larry picked up a piece of bread and ate it, the next day on walking past Larry nicked another piece of bread when suddenly an inmate ran out,

"Give me that bread, Give me that bread."

Larry ate the bread and then punched the guy on the chin and over he went onto the floor, he wasn't hurt but was taken by surprise. Luckily no prison officer saw this incident. Larry was told later by an inmate that the inmate he had punched was Klaus Fuchs, a spy who gave atomic bomb secrets to the Russians. Larry had never heard of him. On reflection nicking another prisoners bread was probably a rotten thing to do, but Larry was starving at the time as was everybody.

Whilst waiting to be transferred from Wormwood scrubs it was back to sewing mailbags, mailbags and more mailbags.

After a short spell in Wormwood scrubs the pair of them were transferred to Hollesley Bay prison in Suffolk. Larry was assigned to one barracks and Robert another in an attempt to keep them apart.

In a strange way Larry enjoyed his time in Borstal, it offered more freedom, the food was decent, it had a good gym and there were many sports to get involved in, football boxing running to name just three. Larry had never had these things in his life before and thought in a way the judge who sentenced him had done him a favour.

Although all prisoners were there to be punished, Larry never saw it as punishment he was having a good time, sitting down to regular meals, having the use of all the facilities, the sports side of things was tremendous. Larry particularly enjoyed boxing although he could fight he had never done any boxing before.

Anyway one day whilst in the gym a guy called Larry up into the ring, this guy just danced around Larry jabbing him here and there, Larry always looking for a knockout punch was getting more and more frustrated so kicked out. The instructor came over immediately and gave him a right rollicking "That's not boxing it's just not on." Larry soon realised that to win he would have to box more tactically rather than going straight for the killer punch, a good lesson was learnt here and it did help him later on in life. A lot of bullying did go on in the barracks, but most people left Larry alone knowing full well he could look after himself. He had proven that both inside and outside of Borstal.

All inmates were assigned jobs initially Larry was given that of a messenger. In the summer months he worked in the orchards, picking various apples, he loved the sense of freedom and saw this time as one of the best in his life. All the apples picked were loaded onto wagons for distribution around the country. The inmates would often give the drivers a few boxes on the quiet in return for contraband, the likes of tobacco, chocolate, sweets and other items they never got in prison. Larry became very friendly with one of the drivers from London, who offered him an escape route, one of his pals was up for this but not Larry, for once in his life he realised how good it was in this prison and thought what is the point, if he escaped and got caught he would be thrown in a rotten stinky old prison and also lose remission. By staying put he would serve his time and hopefully earn some remission, it was doing him no harm at all, he was a better person for it and a lot fitter. Some of the inmates were finding Borstal an unpleasant experience, but not Larry it was a breeze after the hardships he had endured in his life so far. One of his friends was still up for escaping so he took up the drivers offer jumped in the wagon and he was away. Larry gave himself a pat on the back he had shown restraint and knew he only had another 18 months to serve. Besides doing his allocated jobs Larry decided to also take up an optional painting and decorating course, which he did very well in and was a course that would serve him well in later life.

Borstal inmates were encouraged to better themselves education wise. Larry's education had been minimal playing truant all the time he was hardly ever in school. However, it was at school where his artistic talent started to emerge, not that his parents ever recognised it. He would draw all the time at home often sketching on his sister's school books to jazz them up a bit, drawing was a real pleasure to Larry.

So whilst in borstal Larry joined an art class, mainly because the tutor taking the class was a stunning young lady, on one occasion the tutor came over to Larry admiring his work and telling him how good he was. She also asked him if he had ever painted, which he hadn't, so the tutor told him she would supply him with equipment to enable him to paint watercolours. With plenty of encouragement Larry was now painting some really good watercolours, the tutor told him that when he left prison he should keep it up and seek encouragement from his parents, Larry just thought to himself well that isn't going to happen because I know what I am going to do, I am a crook and determined to be one.

Larry always remembered his tutor's words though

"I think you could be a good artist"

How right she was, but that's another story that you will read about further down the line.

After spending about 18 months in borstal Larry was discharged. He was feeling a better person for the experience, was a lot fitter and had a better understanding of life in general whilst still retaining the mischief in his own personality. He was ready for the big wide world again but with a different set of eyes, he realised how many mistakes he had made in the past and for a young man of his age it was far too many. The question was what now? He was up for anything and that would no doubt result in run-ins with the law at some point.

CHAPTER 3

RETURNING HOME / NATIONAL SERVICE

1948

On his release from prison Larry was tempted to head back to London and stay there never returning home again. However, after much thought he decided that returning to his hometown was probably the best move he could take at this point in his life and it would also be good to see his family and friends who still lived in Burnley.

On the train journey back home to Burnley he looked out of the window with a sense of freedom, it was a fantastic feeling but he did wonder how he would be accepted by his family on returning home.

On disembarking the train, he decided to make the rest of the journey home on foot, passing people he knew, the shops he had robbed and seeing the emergence of new buildings. Larry arrived at the family home at about 6 p.m. and with being summer time it was still light outside. He felt anxious as he stood at the front door, he didn't know what to expect, would he be greeted with love or treated as an outcast? Taking a deep breath he tried the front door which was not locked, on entering the house he felt as if he had never been away, nothing had changed. His parents were sat down in the kitchen enjoying a cup of tea, his mother welcomed him home and asked him if he would also like a cup of tea. He sat down at the table with his parents enjoying the tea, it had been a long time since he had had a decent brew. Larry's dad was staring at him, it seemed as though he was weighing him up. Larry not knowing what to expect looked deep in to his dad's eyes and for the first time he thought "Dad really rates me as a son, but I know he won't say so".

After a game of dominoes, his dad said to Larry

"I bet you are glad to be home and I guess you will need to start looking for a job"

Larry knew he needed to find a job, he looked at differing legal options and decided he would take a job offer to work on the local railway which was very close to where he lived. The wages were okay but Larry knew this wasn't a career job, it was only a job to fill in time before he received his call up papers. Whilst working on the railway Larry was tasked with cleaning the engines, moving coal around and many more labouring jobs that were needed. Socially Larry met up with some of his old pals visiting places himself and Robert used to go to before leaving for London. Robert who had been discharged earlier than Larry was fine, but crime was a path he no longer wished to tread, there was no way he was going to end up back in prison, unlike Larry he was not cut out for crime and no longer had the bottle for it anymore.

Larry eventually received his national service call up papers in 1948 and after passing a medical was initially assigned to the East Lancashire Regiment. It was just like being back in borstal, the corporals and sergeants shouting out instructions and orders and eyeballing everyone that came through. Larry didn't know anyone but soon made friends with a couple of young lads. Initial training focussed on fitness and firearms, Larry was already in good shape and thrived on the assault course, but without doubt it felt like being back in prison again with the usual bullies. There was one corporal in particular around 22 years of age who used to pick on people right left and centre. This corporal for some reason was always having a go at one of Larry's friends, shouting at him all the time getting him to do this that and the other, the poor lad could do no right in the eyes of this corporal. Inspections were a living nightmare for him, he was so frightened of being picked upon. On one occasion the corporal, as per usual, picked on this young lad even though there was nothing wrong with his kit and shoes. Larry had had enough of this bullying and told the corporal where to go. The corporal turned around and stared at Larry Saying

"What did you say?" Larry replied

"You heard me first time, forget about who you are, you are nothing but a bully and everyone knows that, when you have finished training get back here and we will see if you are a good bully or a bad one, I am going to have you over"

The corporal replied "Rushton what do you mean"

Larry responded "I am going to have you over"

The corporal responded

"Rushton I was going to put you on a charge, but no I am going to come back tonight and teach you a lesson"

Larry turns away "Please do"

Around 8 p.m. the corporal turns up with a colleague and goes over to Larry

"This is the cheeky bastard Rushton who was mouthing off this morning, what have you got to say for yourself Rushton"

Looking right into the corporal's eyes Larry replied

"Exactly what I said to you this morning, you are nothing but a bully. If you have come here to fight I am ready for you,"

The corporal replied "I am more than ready"

he then asked the other corporal to lock the door.

The pair of them squared up to each other, Larry was thinking to himself, "thanks borstal" this is where I come into my own. As the corporal was throwing punches Larry was ducking and weaving whilst catching him with punches to the ribs and under the guts leaving his face alone completely. All of a sudden the corporal knew he was in for a pasting and as Larry got a bit closer to him the corporal head butted him.

Larry shook it off "I thought we were having a fight"

The corporal responded "I will fight anyway I wish to"

On hearing that Larry landed a powerful punch, with the corporal now doubled up in pain Larry flattened him, he got up and Larry flattened him again. The corporal had had enough by now he was a beaten man.,

In a depth of pain he said to Larry

"Any more of this and I will put you on a court martial"

Larry responded "Any more of what, we had a fair fight and you lost! I have 25 witnesses to back me up."

With this the other lads cheered Larry. The corporal turned to his colleague, questioning what should happen next but the other corporal replied nothing it was a fair fight and you lost. There was no further trouble from that corporal again, job done. Larry's name was now down as that of a trouble maker. Shortly after that incident Larry was moved to Blackdown barracks near Aldershot. He found them to be terrific barracks, and the food was excellent. Whilst there he was approached for a position in the military police, which is quite ironic really, this he duly accepted and even made corporal. Larry did have the opportunity to move up to sergeant but he never studied the courses, as with school studying was never on the agenda for Larry and he consequently failed the exams, losing his stripes in the process. Shortly after this he was moved to Regents barracks London a place where all the staff cars for the military were kept. The activity here was unbelievable, cars were in and out all day. Larry found this a very good posting and it was extremely convenient for nipping into the big city.

It was here he made friends with a guy called James a born and bred Londoner. He had a bit of a past like Larry, having been in borstal and prison so they had much in common. Larry was assigned to the gatehouse due to his experience in the military police here he would check cars in and out. It was here that a petrol scam ensued, the cars would be filled up with petrol and an excess amount poured into jerry cans for selling on. The proceeds would be split with whoever was on the pumps at the time.

If Larry or any of his colleagues wanted to borrow a car they could do so but it was obviously done on the quiet, Larry and James would regularly take out some of the officer's cars without permission. On one occasion they had arranged to pick up a couple of girls they had met earlier that week and thought let's turn up in the General's Bentley. Well they turn up in this Bentley, drinks cabinet fully stocked of course, the look on the girl's faces was a real picture, one of the girl's even dashed into her house for her dad to come and see. Her dad was suspicious but Larry pretended to be a chauffeur. They set off in the car and went for a meal and drinks at a top restaurant, it was a very enjoyable evening but an evening that needed to be cut short as the car had to be returned to the barracks. On the way back the drinks cabinet was put to good use as it was on route to the restaurant, too much so probably as one of the girl's on the way home threw up right over James's head, sick was all over the windscreen, it was absolutely everywhere, in every nook and cranny what a mess.

Larry was now concerned about how they would get the car cleaned up. They dropped the two girls off who were totally hammered by now and then made their way back to the barracks. One of Larry's pals happened to be on duty at the gatehouse and was awaiting their return, but shortly after driving through the entrance a sergeant stopped the car and questioned where they had been.

Larry told the sergeant that they had a taken a Colonel out.

The sergeant said "What's that smell"

Larry replied "The colonel had not been feeling well and threw up in the car so we need to clean it up "

The sergeant was suspicious but Larry got away with it, that sure was a close call. Larry drove the car around the back to where the garages where and the pair of them spent all night cleaning the car. In future they would have to be extremely careful when taking out another car, easier said than done had they really learnt a lesson from that experience.

On another occasion they decided to take a Humber super snipe on a visit to Brighton for the weekend, a trip that would have consequences. The pair of them had plenty of money as a result of the petrol scam and stealing various goods to sell on from the stores, including overcoats, shirts, shoes, so they were heading to Brighton to have a really good time. The pair were having a few good drinks and really enjoying themselves when Larry who was chatting with a young lady suddenly had three local lads standing in front of him, he didn't know what was going on and then he saw James laying straight into one of the lads flattening him before Larry could even talk his way out of the situation. Next minute it all kicked off chairs, ashtrays and any other objects to hand were being used as weapons, it was a blood bath. Heavily outnumbered Larry and James took a real battering, having heard the police had been called they eventually got out of the pub, the landlord had tried to detain Larry but he had no chance. As they made their way back to the car James was now in a really bad way, blood streaming from his head there was no way he could drive back to the barracks. Before setting off, they went to another pub where they cleaned themselves up as best they could. It was now down to Larry who had little experience driving to get them back to the barracks, he was not keen on doing so but had no choice and to make the situation worse being the evening it was dark.

The pair set off James still bleeding from the deep cut on his head, the blood now staining the car seat. Larry had no idea which way to go so had to follow James's instructions. Driving along for one reason or another Larry caught the side of a ditch then collided with a bunch of posts at the side of the road the car ripped all down one side. With only about 20 miles to go they continued to make their way back to the barracks.

As they neared the barracks James said to Larry

“We can’t take the car back in this state we will have to torch it”.

James took his sock off placed it in the petrol filler cap and then lit it, the car went up in flames followed by a terrific explosion, the car was blown all over the place. James had a house nearby, so they slept there for the night.

Arriving back at the barracks the following morning the pal of Larry’s that booked the car out was no longer on duty. Larry asked the guy on duty if the car had been booked out which he confirmed. He then told the guy on duty

“Well it’s not coming back we have blown it up so what are we going to do”

Replying to Larry “I will have to say it has been stolen”

“Well you will have to say that then won’t you, that’s the way we will do it then, I owe you” Larry replied as he walked away.

The barracks were rather strange there was very little discipline people did as they wished, for a few quid you could bribe the officer on rota duty to put you down for some time off. It appeared to be crooked from top to bottom.

CHAPTER 4

COUNTRY MANSION ROBBER

1948 - 1949

James a friend of Larry's stationed in the same barracks was approached by a chauffeur he knew. The chauffer mentioned that he was a driver for one of the Major's, this major was a right playboy who regularly visited a country manor house where he would meet up with a well to do young lady. The chauffeur would drive the Major to the manor house where he would then wait for the Major maybe a few hours or sometimes all night. With so many visits the chauffeur became friendly with the servants who looked after him, from them he learned all the evening routines.

The chauffer approached James

"This manor house is magnificent and a prime place for robbing there is an abundance of antiques, silver, jewellery, fur coats. Have a word with Larry and see if he is interested in taking this place on"

James didn't hesitate "Larry will be no doubt be up for this" he replied.

After speaking to Larry the two of them took one of the less noticeable cars from the barracks and drove up to the mansion to check it out. They arrived at a time when all the guests would have retired to their rooms and were let in the back door by the chauffeur who was on overnight duty on this occasion. The place was amazing, an ideal place to rob but to take it on that evening would not have been a good idea as there may have been implications for the chauffeur. The robbery would need to take place when the chauffeur was off duty, it wouldn't be difficult gaining entry as for whatever reason the mansion's doors were never locked, it was a thief's paradise.

Larry and James now waited on the chauffeur to let them know when he was off duty and when the next big party was to be held. Having been given the nod Larry and James drove up to the mansion, as they approached the mansion there was an array of really top class cars in the driveway and just as the chauffeur had predicted the doors were not locked. It was now around 2.30 in the morning, a few lights were on but everyone had retired to their rooms. The place was now a bit of a tip, it must have been some party, empty bottles of champagne all up and down the place. They took a look around and sure enough in the cloakroom there were many expensive fur coats, and silver items in many of the rooms, they couldn't come back so this was a one-time opportunity. The silver items were put into sacks they found in the kitchen and the coats just bundled into the car.

As they were about to leave with their stash Larry noticed a magnificent landscape painting in the study and thought it may be worth a fortune, James wasn't keen on taking it though, knocking out the coats and silver would be easy but paintings a whole new ball game. Larry agreed but as luck would have it whilst in the study he came across a bundle of notes, jewellery and a gold watch. Larry was well pleased with the goods they had thieved but was now keen to venture upstairs, James was having none of it though far too risky so they left the upstairs well alone.

James knew a Yid who lived in the west end, a fence with a good reputation so they took the stolen silver, coats and jewellery to him. This guy was pleased with the goods and gave them a few quid to be going on with whilst he moved the goods on. A couple of days after the robbery there was a newspaper article covering the mansion robbery, according to the paper a small fortune in silver, jewellery and fur coats had been stolen. Maybe this was true or maybe the owners were just trying to up the insurance claim.

Just over a week after the robbery Larry and James visited the fence to receive the rest of their money. The Yid a very shrewd guy told them the silver was rubbish and the coats not up to much and subsequently gave them a pittance for the goods. Neither Larry nor James were happy about this having read the newspaper article they knew this Yid was having them over.

James said to Larry

"Well Larry at this stage there is not a lot we can do"

Larry replied

"Well I think there is a lot we can do we will ask for the gear back"

They visited the Yid again but he said the goods had already been moved on. Larry was very unhappy and wanted to do him there and then, but James told Larry to just leave it for now. They did receive a few hundred quid but nowhere near what the goods were worth. Larry still brooding told James that they couldn't let him get away with it.

Later that day James said

"We should go back in disguise, tie him up and then rob him".

"James now you're talking, I will have some of that with you" replied Larry

They left it for about 2 weeks then decided to give the Yid a surprise call. James acquired some army tape, really strong tape that was used on cars and for wrapping gear up, so dressed in old overcoats, balaclavas over their heads they paid the Yid a visit, as he opened the door Larry grabbed hold of him wrestling him to the floor, James then gagged him, tied him up and sat him in a chair, not a word was spoken. The pair of them searched the place found a few quid but nothing like what they expected. Larry lifted carpets and floorboards up, slashed a mattress that was upstairs, they searched absolutely everywhere but found nothing. The last option was to search the Yid himself, they went through his jacket and trousers and found nothing but a few quid, so they stripped him down to his underwear and found a leather pouch in his underpants which contained some nice jewellery including diamond rings and emeralds. Having found his stash, they left him in the chair and returned to the barracks, where Larry put the goods in his steel locker. James later on called the police to let them know this Yid was tied up to a chair so they could free him. Quite some time later James saw the Yid who told him about the robbery, he had no idea it had been Larry and himself.

CHAPTER 5

ROBBERY WITH VIOLENCE

1948 - 1949

At this time in their lives both Larry and James were quite flush with money so would treat themselves to quality clothing and in their spare time go out and have a really good time no expense spared. One evening they decided to visit London's west end for a meal and a few drinks, they were sitting in a pub having a right few drinks when a beautiful young girl came in and kept giving James the eye. He wasn't going to miss this opportunity so he went over and bought her a drink, Larry then went over to join them. It turned out she was hooker and this was one of the pubs she used. She gave James a price which was only a few quid and asked him if he wanted to go to back to her place which wasn't far away, he was up for that so he left with her and arranged to meet Larry in the pub in an hour or so.

When the pair of them arrived at her place she asked James to take his clothes off and have a wash in a side room which was just off the bedroom before joining her in the bedroom

When the pair had finished having sex James went to his jacket to pay and found his money had gone, £400. This confused him at first then he realised someone must have done his pocket and nicked it. The hooker was now demanding her money.

James replied “I want my money you have done me”

She denied it all, James was raging and gave her a crack, within seconds a guy suddenly appears from nowhere he was obviously the one who had taken the money so James lays into him too and gives him a right going over, he then took what money she had in her handbag and left the place.

Larry unaware of what had been going on was waiting in the pub when James runs in out of breath and says.

“Larry lets be on our toes we need to get out of here”

James explained what had happened then they left for another pub just down the road. They stayed there for a while before setting off for the barracks, but as they left the pub a police car called pulled up beside them.

The hooker was there screaming

“It was those two, both of them robbed me”

It wasn’t true but the police didn’t want to know, they didn’t believe James’s story and arrested both of them. They were both put on remand in Brixton prison and after a few months were sentenced to 4 years a piece in Wandsworth prison for robbery with violence. This was the one time in his life that Larry was actually innocent they didn’t believe a word of his defence and it was a right kick in the teeth for him and a hard pill to swallow.

Larry now nearing 19 Years of age reflected back on his time in Liverpool prison at the age of 16 and how horrendous it was there, it was like something out of a

Dickins novel everything about the place was grey even the people's faces seemed grey. Wandsworth prison in comparison was much cleaner, a paradise compared to Liverpool.

However, it was a prison where you would be locked up for 23 hours a day with an hours exercise if you were lucky. It was a very strict prison, a prison where the officers just wanted to show their authority and with there being no real checks on prisons during this time the officers used to get away with murder. On one occasion an old prisoner had been giving lip to the officers, later that evening four of them visited his cell, you could hear him screaming as they were kicking the hell out of him. Larry didn't see this old guy until about two months later his face now badly scarred. The brutality given out by the officers was off the scale. Seeing what they had done to this prisoner hurt Larry but he was in no position to do anything about it.

Larry was eventually assigned a job sewing mailbags as was James which was okay as it got them out of their cell for a while and gave them a little more freedom. They couldn't really talk to each other though as again the rule was no talking whilst working, if you did you would be taken before the governor and maybe given two days' bread and water, so you really just had to shut up and say nothing.

During their time in Wandsworth James received several visits whilst Larry received none and to be honest he didn't really want any anyhow. It was now time to be moved on and the pair of them were transferred to Lewes prison in Suffolk, Larry had never heard of this place and thought well I will definitely receive no visits now as this prison is a long long way from home. They eventually arrived at Lewes prison, it was a very old Victorian prison and in some ways resembled a castle. The cells were small again as it was one to a cell. The landings had suicide nets for those who tried to throw themselves over. Whilst here Larry was once again assigned to sewing mailbags, he never seemed to get a decent job. James ended up working in the kitchens. One good thing about the prison was its sports field, physical training and six a side football was always something to look forward to. However, in charge of the sports were two officers who reminded Larry of peacocks strutting around with their chests stuck out and hands behind their backs, they were two real bullies who would have a go at you for the slightest thing you did wrong. One young lad in there was continually taunted by one of the officers and a fight ensued for which he was punished by being put on bread and water.

CHAPTER 6

LEWES PRISON - A GHOSTLY ENCOUNTER

1950 - 1953

With Lewes prison being a young offenders prison inmates were only imprisoned here until they reached the age of 21, on reaching 21 they would then be transferred to another prison. The majority of prison officers here were ex-military and were very arrogant, on arrival they immediately let you know who was boss, they had a right attitude about them and just wanted to give you the hardest time possible, real bullies who just wanted to shout orders and give you a whack. It was important to keep cells clean and tidy as the prison officers were always trying to find fault at the regular inspections. One of the physical training officers (will be referred to as Prick 1) was always picking on someone and was by far the worst.

Many of the young inmates in Lewes prison moved on to become major criminals, one in particular was Ronnie Biggs (Great Train Robbery of 1963) who was in the next but one cell to Larry. Larry remembered Ronnie well because on Larry's 21st birthday he went to the toilet to slop out as he did every morning and on returning to his cell his smoking tin which had a little tobacco and some roll up papers in it had disappeared. Larry was convinced that when it was

Ronnie's turn to slop out he had visited Larry's cell first and nicked the tin. Biggs had to be the culprit he was a cunning, mischievous person a right weasel. Larry was having another look around his now locked cell for the tin when he heard a tinkling noise from outside, on looking out of his cell window he could see his tin in the courtyard below. Later on when the cells were re-opened for work Larry nipped into Ronnie's cell to confront him about stealing the tin, Ronnie denied it of course, Larry was going to give him a dig but he was that good at lying he now had Larry believing him. Larry went all down the line of cells confronting the other inmates but they all denied seeing or even taking the tin. A lesson was learnt here never leave anything in your cell, be a bit sharper and trust no one.

That was a good start to Larry's 21st, his tobacco had been nicked and he had to spend it alone in his cell, no cards, letters or anything were received. In later years when on the outside Larry would have an inner smile when he saw people celebrating their 21st birthday, it brought back vivid memories of his 21st spent in Lewes prison.

Trouble was now beginning to brew between Larry and an inmate called Johnny who was always taking the piss out of him, Larry used to take it as a bit of a joke but it was getting beyond that now so Larry asked him to pack it in otherwise he would set about him, Johnny welcomed the confrontation. A prison officer called Joe had noticed something was going on, there had been nothing physical as yet but he noticed the raised voices and the growing tension. After a while Joe decided to intervene and put an end to this bad feeling and tension so he took both Larry and Johnny to one side, led them into a store room and asked them if they wanted to sort it out here and now, Johnny was well up for it so Larry not one to back down thought I will have to now and agreed. A fight ensued both of them giving as good as they were getting.

After a while Joe said "That's enough you have had a right go, now shake hands and your pals"

Larry agreed and the pair shook hands. The officer thought this would be an end to problem, but Larry could tell by the look in Johnny's eyes that this was not over.

Not long after this incident Larry was walking in the courtyard, the drill there would be one group of prisoners walking clockwise and another group walking anti clockwise. There would be about 300 prisoners walking around at any one time with prison officers strategically placed to keep an eye on things. Well on this particular day Larry was walking around with James and a couple of other inmates when he saw Johnny walking towards him with a couple of his pals, as Johnny got level he gave Larry a right dig, knocking him backwards, regaining his balance Larry steamed into him they were having a right ding dong when a whistle was blown and officers intervened, the pair of them were led away to the punishment block and brought before the governor. The governor had warned Larry before about his bad attitude and fighting so not only was he given seven days' solitary confinement in a punishment cell he was also put on bread and water and lost some remission.

The punishment cells were in the depths of the prison in two rows about ten on either side. As Larry was taken down to the cells the prison officers were waiting, like a bully mob, including the officer he hated most 'Prick 1'.

On the way to his cell which was more like a dungeon, Larry was handed out some brutal punishment, he was getting kicked everywhere and took a really good battering with 'Prick 1' telling the other officers what to do. As Larry was thrown into his cell one of the officers said "We will make sure you know you are down here and it's the best place for you". One on one they were spineless but together just a bunch of bullies.

In the morning after slopping out Larry would be given a piece of bread and as much water as he wanted. Sometimes for a joke the bread would be covered in salt but you were so hungry you would eat anything, on other occasions they would throw the bread at you as if you were an animal. In solitary breakfast was bread and water for 4 days then 3 days on porridge, lunchtime a boiled potato and some slop and then in the evening just bread and water.

Whilst in this dread awful cell Larry sitting on a chair in the middle of his cell was back to sewing mailbags again. Apart from the prison officers the only other person he would see was a cleaner who each morning came down to clean the outside of the cells, passageways and the toilets.

On one occasion Larry whispered to the cleaner.

"Any chance of a rollup"

The cleaner replied

"I will leave one in your blankets"

The blankets were always kept outside during the day and prisoners would bring them into the cells of an evening when a bell rang. The blankets were placed on a dirty thin mattress which lay on the steel beds. This rollup was to be a real treat, a highlight of the day, but it quickly turned into a living nightmare. Larry looking so forward to this rollup neatly folded up his clothes and placed them on his solitary chair which was in the middle of the cell, being neat and tidy was something he had picked up during his service time. He then sat down on his bed to enjoy the rollup, a small moment of pleasure.

This pleasure was short lived though, as he sat on his bed just starting to enjoy the rollup he felt a strong presence in the cell whilst also noticing from the corner of his eye an indentation being made on his neat pile of clothes, it was as if someone was sitting down pushing down on them. Larry in his own words had never been so shocked and frightened in his life, he didn't know what to do then suddenly he kicked the chair over, picked the steel bed up and battered it against the cell door. He hadn't been on any drugs and was not hallucinating, this was for real and extremely frightening, Larry completely lost it, he was banging on his cell door to try and get an officer's attention.

Eventually an officer heard the commotion and made his way down to the cells he looked through the spy hole of Larry's cell and asked him what the hell was going on why was he making such a racket.

Larry was screaming

"You have got to get me out of here, you have got to get me out of here I have seen something".

The officer told him

"Get your head down, shut up and stop banging"

Larry carried on banging away.

The officer once again warned him

"Stop now or we will come in and batter you".

Larry replied

"I wish you would".

Larry carried on, he bent the steel bed and the door, the whole cell was smashed up, he was behaving like a lunatic. The officer was now worried and with three other officers now beside him opened the cell door. Larry flew at them, he needed to get out of there he was petrified.

"You can do what you want to me but there is no way I am going back into that cell".

The officers saw the state Larry was in and must have then realised they weren't going to get him back in the cell so after giving him a good kicking they eventually moved him into another cell further down, with no blankets or anything. After an unexpected decent night's sleep Larry reflected on what may have happened if they had left him in the cell, he was that scared he may even have done himself in.

For this incident Larry was on report and brought before the prison governor, no one believed his story they thought he was off his head. As he was already on maximum punishment Larry just lost further remission. The governor asked Larry if he had any more to say.

Larry replied

"I have seen something in that cell and all the punishment you can give me in the world will not be as bad as staying in that cell".

Did they now maybe believe a little and was the incident recorded? Larry was then taken back down to another cell.

An inmate having heard rumours about that evening was concerned about Larry he therefore spoke to a priest 'Father Flanagan' and asked if he would be kind enough to visit Larry, this he duly did. The priest was a very nice man, who Larry knew from going to Bible classes, many inmates attended these so they spent more time away from their cell.

Well, the priest was shocked to see the state Larry was in, how badly hurt he was and after hearing Larry's story complained to the Governor about the way Larry had been treated. The governor was not interested and told the priest to stick to his own job religion and leave punishment to himself.

The time had now come for James to be transferred from Lewes prison to Pentonville prison to complete the remaining few months of his sentence. It was a sad day for Larry as he missed James his best pal as you always needed someone like that beside you in prison. Larry never saw James again but heard that a few years after his release he became involved in an argument over a woman and was stabbed to death on the side of a pavement and left to die, a sad end for someone so young, maybe it was his growing reputation of being a hard man that brought a blade into the picture. Larry believed that if this incident had not happened he would of no doubt of gone on to be a major criminal he had everything in his locker, the personality, courage, a good outlook and the right connections.

Meanwhile Larry was still getting into trouble in Lewes prison, nothing major, he was just being too lippy and not doing as he was told. On one occasion the officer Larry despised most Prick 1 was giving him a hard time so Larry being Larry told him in no uncertain terms what he thought of him and for this he was brought before the governor again. Prick 1 was relaying the incident, much of it lies, but it made no difference he received a further two weeks' solitary confinement.

It was back to the chair in the middle of the cell sewing mailbags once again. To strengthen the mailbags black wax would be used on the thread, well one day for one reason or another Larry set about sketching on the cell wall with this black wax, he drew a chariot race, warriors, romans killing each other and the like. It turned into a big mural Larry really got carried away with it and was having some great fun for a change. The following morning the governor with a chief officer came down to check on the inmates, Larry knew his turn was coming and stood to attention in the doorway as was the custom. As the cell door opened the governor's eyes strayed over Larry's shoulder he was looking at the mural that had been drawn on white wall.

The governor remarked

"Good god who has done that"

Larry replied

"I am afraid it was me Governor, you get a bit fed up in solitary"

The governor commented

"What are you doing in here when you can do stuff like this you should be an artist. you really are a fool"

the governor then closed and locked the cell door before leaving.

The next morning Larry was on report and brought before the governor once again, although he had praised the mural Larry had sketched on the cell wall he was to be punished for defacing the wall, seven days' loss of remission and a further three days' solitary. Larry smiled thinking to himself it was a whitewash wall with specks of blood all over it, it needed decorating. Larry returning to his cell was not amused so he decided to continue drawing within the cell, every wall was sketched on, he depicted the governor's face on a little scared weakling being chased up and down by romans.

Larry wondered if the governor ever saw that cell again after what he had done to it. The following morning an officer came down to move Larry to another cell, seeing what was on the walls, he called a fellow officer to come and take a look, they both had a smile on their faces as they moved Larry on but warned him not to do anything similar or he would be in for a good kicking. Sat in his new cell sewing mailbags once again Larry had a wry smile on his face as he thought about the mural which by now would have been whitewashed over.

The day came when Larry was once again brought before the governor but this time it was due to him being transferred to Wandsworth prison as at 21 years of age he was no longer classed as a young offender.

The governor said

“I will be glad to see the back of you Rushton, there is real rebellious side to you, and rebels don’t go down well in this prison”

Larry actually enjoyed the journey to Wandsworth it was the first time he had been on the outside for quite some time, to see the world again felt really good. As with previous prisons Larry was once again assigned to sewing mailbags, he must have been an expert by now. In Wandsworth Larry kept his head down and managed to serve the remainder of his sentence without getting into any further trouble, maybe because in Wandsworth he felt as though he had been treated more like an adult, there was no personal bullying as there had been in Lewes.

CHAPTER 7

PRISON DISCHARGE / BLACKPOOL - GOLDEN MILE

1953

The day finally arrived in 1953 when Larry was discharged with just £5 to his name. On walking out of the prison gates Larry looked up at the sky it was such a wonderful feeling he felt human again. He was now able to walk freely leaving behind the dirty brick walls, the iron doors banging behind him, people shouting at him, the noise of people screaming whilst being beaten, the smell of stale food and the stink of sweat which had been in the mattresses for donkey's years as in those days it was only one bath or shower a week. People talk about smelling freedom, Larry now knew what they were talking about because he could smell it too. As Larry embraced his freedom his thoughts turned to what he may have been missing.

Larry free once again decided he would head for Blackpool as he had a brother and sister living there and at least he would have a place to sleep. So with only the clothes on his back and a fiver in his pocket he boarded a train for Blackpool where he shared a carriage with four other people, there was a couple munching sandwiches in the corner, an old man who had fallen asleep directly opposite him and a young girl a little further down. As the journey progressed Larry was looking forward to having a good time but only had a fiver to get buy on, well that was about to change very quickly.

As the journey progressed the couple and young girl who were sharing the carriage disembarked at stations prior to Blackpool leaving Larry and the old man sleeping opposite him alone in the carriage. Larry noticed this guy had removed his jacket with it being a warm day, placing it on the seat next to himself. Larry was now sensing an opportunity, having just been discharged from prison a few hours earlier he was about to break the law again, he had lost none of his bottle whatsoever he leant over and dipped the old man's pocket removing a wallet which he took to the toilets. Larry was surprised it contained £70, having taken the cash he made his way back to the carriage to return what was now an empty wallet, luckily the old man was still asleep. As the train was now approaching Blackpool Larry moved further down the train to disembark, now £75 better off which was a lot of money in 1953. On leaving the train Larry signalled a taxi and headed for his brother's home which he shared with his wife. They were both pleased to see him and truly looked after him. What a change from prison he had a comfy bed to sleep in and the daily use of a bathroom. He also enjoyed the meals cooked by his sister-in-law, food had never tasted so good after what he had been used to whilst in prison. With his brother and sister–in-law working during the day Larry had the run of the house. However, Larry realised he could not live with them indefinitely and would need to find a job then a place of his own to live.

So in need of a job Larry headed for Blackpool's golden mile, he was weighing up all the stalls when he came across a photographer's stall which took photos of people as they walked down the golden mile, or as they stood next to a caricature or put their head through one of the holes to look like King Charles or other characters. Larry approached the owner of the stall a gentleman call Vic to see if there were any jobs going. Vic outlined the job which was basically persuading people to have their photo taken which would be processed for a fee and be available to pick up later that day or the following morning. Larry had no experience but Vic was impressed with him and told him if he smartened himself up he would give him a job on a standard weekly wage with a bonus incentive. The hours were long, most days eleven in the morning until midnight, but Larry was now a photographer and got real a buzz out of meeting new people every day, this was his first real job and he was really enjoying it. The holiday makers normally came down for a week or two and were hard working people who were out to enjoy themselves and they truly did, the golden mile was real hub of activity. Most of the time the photos were ready to be picked up the same day or the following day but if business was really good that was not always the case and that's when trouble used to start, some of them wanted their money back and wouldn't take no for an answer, even though the photos would have been mailed to them when processed. Vic's rule was no refunds, this led to Larry being involved in numerous fights as some of the harder guys and those that had been drinking would take a pop at him. Larry recalled the fights as being some of the best fights of his life. On one occasion during a Scottish weekend an incident involving a donkey with a rubber head took place, this donkey was by the stall and people would have their photo taken with it. Well on one occasion a real drunken brute of a man wanted his photo taken sitting on the donkey. As he was sat on the donkey he suddenly pulled out what looked like a hunting knife and cut the donkeys head off, screaming

"I've killed the fucking donkey, a Blackpool donkey".

Larry and Kath who also worked on the stall looked at each other then quickly gathered the day's takings before running for it with this drunken idiot pursuing them with the large knife. The drunk shouted at them,

"Come back, come back a want my photo taken".

This was one time Larry wasn't hanging around he was a raving lunatic.

After finishing work for the day Larry often used to witness many group fights on the golden mile and in the surrounding pubs, alcohol fuelled it was always kicking off, even the police took a battering at times.

Out of prison life back on the streets was good every day a different experience it was amazing. Larry was having just a great time and felt so privileged to be working on the golden mile, it was like paradise after being in prison and with the job going so well Larry was earning good money and could now afford to move into a flat of his own.

CHAPTER 8

BLACKPOOL CRIMINALS / SAFE BREAKING

1953 - 1957

With the Blackpool summer season now over Larry was only working whilst the Blackpool illuminations were on, in his eyes with everywhere lit up it was like working in a poor man's Las Vegas. His days were mostly free to do as he wished as he wouldn't start work until five in the evening and then on into the early hours of the morning. Larry enjoyed working the summer season in Blackpool followed by the Blackpool illuminations, he met so many different characters and not one day was the same. However, as with all good things they come to an end eventually and this was the case for Larry, when the illuminations period finished so did his job, Blackpool became a ghost town. The money he saved during the summer months would soon disappear so it was time to find a new job for the winter.

With Larry's only experience prior to working on the golden mile being that of a criminal, it was time to get back to his old tricks, it was all he knew.

When Larry initially arrived in Blackpool he didn't really know anyone and he now needed to mingle with people who were on his own wave length. He did make a few acquaintances during the summer jack the lad type of characters who would earn their money buying and selling knock off gear, guys who could always lend their hand to something. The Blackpool hangout where all these guys used to meet up was referred to as the 'Iron lung' an old Joe Davis snooker hall, the reason it was called the 'Iron Lung' was due to the fact it was always full of smoke. Walking through the doors you would be met by what could only be described as a fog which was down to the endless smoking of cigarettes and cigars. Gambling was also rife, betting on horse racing, greyhound racing and playing cards being the most popular activities. The 'Iron Lung' may have been a snooker hall by name but in truth it was without doubt the place to go for those with criminal tendencies, it was a breeding ground for the criminal fraternity, a place to meet criminals and build up a network of useful contacts. With there being no wire taps or likewise tracking tools around this time these professional criminals worked with quite a bit of freedom.

Larry was now surrounded by many criminals, and listening to their stories and antics gave him a real buzz an urge to get back in the game. His criminal contacts list and network was growing by the day. Whilst in the 'Iron Lung' playing snooker and sinking a few spirits one evening Larry was approached by a man who went by the name of 'Gelignite Pete' a safe blower from Manchester whom he got on extremely well with.

Gelignite Pete would line up places with safes to rob but as he was getting on in years and not as agile as he used to be he needed help, this is where Larry would come in, he would do the dirty work climbing drainpipes, crossing roofs, whatever was required to break in to a property allowing gelignite Pete to stroll in at his leisure.

On one occasion gelignite Pete had lined up a job in Manchester it was at an old mill where he had been informed that on a certain night of the week there would be a lot of money to be had, a few thousand quid which was a lot of money in the 1950's. Larry's role was to provide transport and break in by climbing up to the 3rd floor via a couple of roofs, the windows on floors one and two were barred, whereas on the third floor they weren't. On arriving at the mill Larry's agility was put to the test as, he made his way up to the third floor via a couple of roofs, he did a window in and then opened a door for Gelignite Pete.

Once inside the mill they found the safe they had been looking for in an office, it was enormous, this didn't worry Gelignite Pete in the slightest, it would be no problem for him he was just going to have to blow both locks on the safe simultaneously. To deaden the noise they needed some packing around the safe, with being a mill there was plenty of material available which they used to pack around the safe this would surely kill most of the noise. Gelignite Pete got to work on the safe, firstly he took off a big brass plate, packed gelignite into the two locks and then wired up the detonator. With all the setting up done the safe was successfully blown, inside it there were many documents and lots of wage packets. So the pair of them made a right few quid out of the robbery, this was a first for Larry a totally new experience.

After this success Larry used to travel around with Gelignite Pete, he would drive him to wherever an opportunity lay which was mainly around the Manchester and Leeds areas. The two of them worked well together and even though they were not making fortunes they were picking up a few grand here and there.

After seeing Gelignite Pete blow a few safes Larry fancied a shot at this himself, getting hold of the gelignite wire and detonators was relatively easy as Larry had become pally with a quarry man in Scotland who used all the gear needed in the quarry for breaking up big stones. Larry was about to get his first opportunity, a pal of Larry's was telling him about a safe in a butchers where the owner kept all his cash, it looked ripe for the taking. The problem with this safe was that they couldn't just take it away as it was concreted into the wall. With many safes it was relatively easy to take them away then with a big pick or chisel and hammer make a hole in the back so that the rivets could be popped off with a crowbar.

Larry's accomplice had his concerns about blowing the safe but Larry was confident after seeing Pete perform the task many times and told him it wouldn't be a problem, no problem at all. The main issue was accessing the safe without being seen as the shop had no window blinds or coverings of any sort and there were people living next door and also across the road from the shop. They would also have to find a way of reducing the noise from the blast somehow. It was certainly going to be tricky but the job was on, Larry broke into the shop through the backdoor carrying all the gear needed then crept under the counter to assess the safe, it was big maybe around forty inches high.

Larry was thinking to himself this will be fine even though he hadn't blown a safe on his own before. Larry's accomplice had no idea, he thought Larry had previously blown a few safes on his own. This being Larry's first attempt at blowing a safe the question was how much gelignite to use? Pete never let him see exactly what he was doing, so making a best guess he opted for two sticks of gelignite, having removed the brass plate from around the keyhole he wedged the gelignite into the keyhole and then attached the wire and detonator. They knew the noise needed to be reduced so the pair of them thought the only thing they could do was to pack meat around the safe, beef, pork, lamb, sausages anything that was to hand, they then moved into a backroom as far away as possible. The pair of them were bricking it both still concerned about the noise, and to be honest Larry maybe more so with this being his first attempt, but on the other hand it also gave him a real buzz too. Well their fears were well founded, there was an almighty bang and the safe was blown right out into the street, just lying there smoking away, too much gelignite by any chance? There was no time to hang around the pair of them legged it down the street as fast as they could. Now feeling relatively safe they looked back down the street, the police had arrived wondering what the hell had gone on, a smoking safe in the middle of the street with lumps of meat strewn absolutely everywhere. Yes, definitely too much gelignite.

A few days after this failed attempt Larry caught up with Gelignite Pete and relayed the story, Pete just laughed his head off he said you are lucky you didn't bring the building down and kill yourselves, next time think of the size of Oxo cubes, an amount of gelignite equal to two Oxo tubes per lock should be ample. Larry always looked on this event as a very amusing moment in his life, the safe in the middle of the street surrounded by lumps of meat with the Police not knowing what to make of it at all. This first attempt was certainly a learning experience.

The type of villainy and thieving Larry was into at this time relied heavily on quality information which was never 100%, nothing was ever certain, some of the safes were just full of documentation no money at all. Some people would provide a tip off for a percentage cut never knowing if they were right, they were just chancers. It was around this time that Larry met a guy called George who had really good connection in Paris. Larry was introduced to one of them when he was visiting the UK. He was introduced because George wanted Larry to take some gear over to Paris, which he did, jewellery in the main, it was a lot easier in those days when security was not as stringent.

Larry made many trips to Paris over the years and was earning good money, business done he would be taken out for meals and to the Paris night clubs. Larry always remembered the smell of pot it was rife in the gangster clubs. The Paris connection was major league a top fence with contacts all over Europe. Larry also became involved with him in taking paintings over to Paris, he would paint a watercolour over a masterpiece to make it look worthless and then once in Paris the watercolour would be washed off.

Another contact Larry made friends with was Jimmy from the Glasgow slums, he was in need of a bit of muscle to support him and thought Larry would be ideal. Larry referred to him as a magpie as he travelled up and down the country nicking anything that looked valuable, parker pens, overcoats, anything really but specialised in transistor radios which were all the rage at the time. The pair of them travelled all over Larry would mind the door whilst Jimmy did the thieving, it was all pretty straight forward really they were making decent money and so far they did not have to resort to violence of any kind. On returning home maybe after being away for a week or so Jimmy would always immediately nip upstairs to hide his money, his wife Diane who was a bit of a lunatic would listen to his every foot step. Jimmy would always hide some money that he knew his wife would find but not the big stash. His wife was truly crazy they were always having parties at which she would get sloshed, and her party trick was to paint on the faces of anyone who fell asleep.

One memorable occasion whilst in London involved a tobacconist shop, Jimmy had been in there and had noticed the shopkeepers coat was hung up just round the corner from the counter and he considered this to be an opportunity not to be missed. The plan was for Larry to distract the shopkeeper whilst Jimmy nicked the wallet from his jacket. With the two of them in the shop Larry asked to see a lighter which was displayed in the window, the shopkeeper came from behind the counter to show him, this was Jimmy's opportunity he pocketed the wallet, all seemed to be going well when the shopkeeper quite a big guy turned around ran at Jimmy grabbing hold of him. Jimmy who was tall but rather skinny was bricking it he was no fighter. The shopkeeper had obviously seen Jimmy's reflection in the shop window and seen what he was up to, time for Larry to step in, a quick tap on the shopkeeper's shoulder and then as he turned around Larry head butted him, the pair of them then legged it back to their car before help was called for. There were numerous incidents following that one where Larry had to get Jimmy out of trouble. Larry found him a pleasure to work with as he was such a top thief and was saddened by his death. Jimmy unfortunately came to a sad end when he was driving back from a Blackpool club with his wife in his big American car, on leaving a roundabout he hit a high kerb crashed the car and killed himself.

Larry at this stage of his Life was now well into safes and worked with a pal of his called Brian and one or two other guys from Manchester. Working on information received they would pull out the safes make a hole in the back and then prise the backs off. The safes inner box would always be fireproofed, sometimes lined with chalk and sand to protect the contents but once the inner box of a safe had been reached it was easy pickings. One pal of Larry's always used a blow torch to cut the safe back off but too many times the contents were set on fire and the money burnt. Gelignite was always the best option but also the most expensive.

One tip off from a reliable source was to do with an engineering works, a big Victorian building, with no bars on the windows, no alarms and assurances there would be no night watchman. The information was that there was a small safe in the building which contained a right few quid. Well on breaking into the building a massive safe was encountered it looked like a seven-foot milliner, but working on the information given it was a small safe which contained the money, therefore the pair of them continued searching until they found the safe. Safe found they took out all the gear they brought with them and set to work on it, but this safe was proving particularly difficult to take the back off. As they worked away trying to open the safe all of sudden a night watchman turns, up bellowing

"What the hell is going on here"

Apparently he had been sleeping further down the building and had turned his light off.

The problem was he had now seen them, Larry's mate ran towards the night watchman and pinned him down, Larry covered his face with his shirt so as not to reveal his identity and then proceeded to tie the guy up with some old rope and net curtains they found lying around, he was then sat in a chair in the corner of the room facing the wall. Apart from being tied up no harm came to the old fella. As referred to earlier information was never 100%, so the night watchman was a total surprise but that wasn't going to be the only surprise. Larry quizzed the night watchman as to what was held in the safe, but he had no idea and muttered

"This is the first time anyone has broken in here".

Three hours later the safe was open they had finally got the back off to find nothing in it but paperwork this break in had been a complete waste of time.

The night watchman was quite upset by now, Larry approached him saying

"I know you are upset but we are going to have to leave you tied up, but I will loosen the ties a bit so you will be able free yourself eventually and here is a few quid for you".

The cash seemed to cheer him up and Larry was confident he would not be identified as the guy only caught a quick glimpse of him before covering his face. So that was really great information, the only person getting any money out of it was the night watchman.

Having found no money in the small safe Larry, didn't want to be beaten and decided he was going to go back and have a go at the big safe, but this time gelignite would be required, so Larry and his pal travelled up to Scotland spent a couple of nights there and came back with the gear they needed. The following week they travelled back to the engineering works to do the big safe. Larry's pal was concerned about there being a night watchman there again, but Larry wasn't bothered if the guy was there again or if somebody else was in his place they would just tie him up, he wasn't going to let a night watchman put him off. Larry had been dreaming about this huge green glossy safe all week and the bottom line was he was going to do it no matter what. Having arrived at the engineering works the pair of them with stockings over their faces this time broke in the same way as last time and were surprised that security hadn't been tightened up. Once inside they came across the same night watchman fast asleep Larry woke the old guy up who was startled and in a trembling voice said

"What do you want, what do you want?

Larry replied

"It's me again we broke in before and gave you a few quid"

The night watchman replied

"The police are looking for you"

Larry laughed

"They will be that's their job, anyway I have come back to blow the big safe, and will bung you a few quid again"

"Really I could do with some more money". Replied the night watchman who was now feeling more comfortable with the situation.

"Can I make you a brew?" he said

Larry thinking he may be up to something replied

"I will make you one you can have it with your sandwiches"

Having had a brew the night watchman was tied up and once again put in a corner facing away from what was going on. It was now time to take on the big safe Larry got to work, taking off the brass plates and remembering what gelignite Pete had told him about 2 Oxo cubes. Larry wished Pete was there as he had not blown a safe such as this one before, and was feeling rather nervous as he proceeded to pack the locks, wire up the detonator then surrounded the safe with curtains to deafen the noise. It was time to go for it and so as not to injure or maybe even kill the night watchman they thought they had better move him into a back office. You could tell this guy was feeling nervous, his eyes watering he said

"Good luck lads, hope there's plenty in the safe"

Moments later a loud bang and the safe was open, Larry was so chuffed with himself and felt a million dollars, he wished he could have captured this moment on camera. Bingo, there was few grand in the safe.

Larry's pal also feeling good about their reward said

"I didn't know you were that good Larry"

Larry just looked at him and smiled.

Before leaving Larry gave the old man a few hundred pounds and told him to hide it somewhere before the police arrived, if he had money on him they may think he was an accomplice. The night watchman was feeling quite happy with his unexpected windfall. Everyone was happy this time.

CHAPTER 9

THE SET-UP

1957

Larry's life was now falling into a particular pattern he would spend his summer months working on Blackpool's golden mile for Vic, a job he really did enjoy and in the winter months it would be back to his criminal activities.

At the age of 24 he was introduced to a couple who had come down from London, Sid and his wife June. Sid was a bit of a wheeler dealer and ran many auction rooms, but the goods were not all that they were made out to be as many customers found out when unpacking their purchases. Sid was making a lot of money mainly from fancy goods that he bought wholesale.

Larry, would hang around with the couple down in the "Iron Lung" and was sure Sid's wife June a very attractive young lady fancied him. He was right it was not long before June got in touch with Larry and they started an affair, but he was sure he was not the only person she was having an affair with. Larry was about to learn a lesson.

Sid contacted Larry about a possible burglary, it was going to be a house in the country, as the two talked Larry was sure Sid knew about the affair but Sid said nothing. The pair of them drove out to the house to assess the job, it looked relatively easy so they scheduled the robbery for the following Sunday. Larry had acquired all the gear required for the robbery and said goodbye to a girl he was knocking around with at the time. Larry shouted to her

"See you later will be back in about 3 hours".

Larry and a friend of his Riley went to meet Sid who was going to be driving them up to the house. On reaching the house Sid thought it best if he remained in the car which was now parked at the end of the driveway whilst Larry and Riley looked for a way in. Entering the property was straight forward enough they just put a downstairs window through. The pair of them then searched the property for a safe which they eventually found in an office. Larry then got to work on the safe in the usual manner, it was ready to be blown or was it, something caught Larry's eye as he looked out of one of the windows he wondered whether he was seeing things, the moonlight was casting shadows but these shadows were moving in the trees, suddenly he saw a copper and shouted to Riley

"We need to get out of here, coppers are moving in "

The pair of them made a run for it, Larry ran through the grounds and jumped over a wall with most of the police in pursuit of him, Larry could run but so could these coppers and they brought him down and cuffed him, he was nicked. Riley had run back towards where the car had been parked but it was gone, however, he did manage to flee the scene.

Larry now realised without a doubt that he was facing more porridge, the police found the gear which he had left behind as the two of them fled the scene, the police had all the evidence they needed. The police questioned Larry as to who his accomplice was but he constantly denied having one, the police knew he was lying but he kept to his story.

Larry was thinking to himself, well I guess I have had a good run, a few good years it's just one of those things and I will have to get on with it. Larry appeared before a magistrate who committed him to crown court for trial. In the mean time Riley was nicked, the police stated that they had seen the two of them driving towards the property on the night in question and followed them. Many of the police were bent in those days and would think nothing of bending the truth to get a conviction and this is what they did to put Riley in the frame. With the events that took place that night Larry was sure Sid had set them up after finding out what was going on with his wife he therefore contacted a pal of his and asked him to do a little digging. Larry's suspicions were confirmed it was indeed Sid who had set them up. Larry learnt a valuable lesson here never mix business with pleasure.

In crown court 1957 both Larry and Riley pleaded guilty to attempted robbery and were sentenced to 3 years each. This time Larry was off to Manchester prison for another spell inside, as with Lewes prison the prison officers would get away with murder, literally, they could do anything they wanted and get away with it. One of the inmates in there was regularly used as punch bag they were just bullies in Larry's eyes.

Whilst in Manchester prison one of the officers kept needling Larry until he finally cracked, swearing a torrent of abuse at the officer, for this he was reported to the governor. It didn't seem to matter which prison you were in the governors all seemed the same, starched shirt waistcoat, brylcreem hair strutting around like a peacock whilst protected by two officers.

The governor questioned why he was being so abusive and telling one of his officers to fuck off.

Larry replied

"You are quite right I did tell him to fuck off and I don't regret it because he needed telling".

The Governor asked Larry if he made a habit of doing this

"Yes I do and you can fuck off too".

It was back to solitary confinement for Larry and as per usual, on his way down to the punishment cell he was punched and kicked in the face and body many times. He was thrown into his cell and called a dirty rat, this cell was dreadful, cold, damp, blood splattered all over the walls.

Larry thought to himself, I can cope with this I have done it before. The trouble was they didn't always feed you and if questioned about it they would say you had refused the food for which you would also get extra punishment. It was going to be harder than Larry expected. Whilst in this cell he was struggling with a very sore throat, he had always had problems with his throat but this was bad really bad, besides having a sore throat he was now sweating profusely and feeling extremely weak. He couldn't eat anything and was just living off water.

The next day the governor paid a visit to Larry's cell

"Everything all right Rushton?"

Larry could hardly speak but replied with a simple "yes."

The following day he visited again

"Everything all right Rushton?"

Larry responded "No I don't feel too good".

The governor just shut the cell door and said

"Well we will see about that"

The following day he visited again

"Everything all right Rushton?"

This time Larry just sat on his bed he couldn't speak he was in a really bad way his throat was badly swollen with puss coming out of it, he was too weak to stand and his whole body was shaking, he felt as though he may have pneumonia. The Governor shouted at him telling him to stand up in front of him, but Larry was too weak to do so.

The following day a prison officer visited Larry's cell, he was one with a bit of decency in him he could see how ill Larry was and decided he would have to go to the prison hospital. Too weak to stand Larry was put on a stretcher and taken to hospital, where a doctor gave him some medication. Larry heard the doctor telling one of the officers that if he had left Larry in his cell for another day he would have been dead. Whilst in the hospital he was visited two or three times a day. So close to dying, this one decent prison officer had actually saved his life.

Shortly after this near death experience Larry was transferred to Lancaster Prison. It was a ferocious place and even though he was now closer to Blackpool he received no family visits, an occasional letter but no visits. He just felt like a he was a loner.

This prison was like a medieval castle, not a bad place, nowhere near as brutal as Manchester and the food was much better. It was quite a relief to have to complete the remaining two years of his sentence here, not bad at all.

Whilst in Lancaster though he was approached by a con who was talking about breaking out, the locks on the doors were so old fashioned that you could use a piece of string to fire the locks back, he relayed his escape plan to Larry who was well up for it. The plan was to attempt the escape around 6 p.m. when it was dark they would make their way through the courtyard then open a couple of doors which would lead them to the main wall and office blocks. Larry asked him if he was sure they could get out that way, the con told him it wouldn't be a problem. Larry packed what little possessions he had, he was ready to go ahead with the escape only for this con to back out making an excuse that his wife was visiting him in a couple of days and he wanted to talk it over with her first. Larry was far from happy but was ready to go so decided to attempt the escape himself. He made his way through the courtyard and got through the gates he needed to by using a lace to spring the locks. Once through the gates he emerged in another courtyard and couldn't believe what he saw, the walls were massive, there was no way he was getting over those walls not what he was expecting to be faced with at all. It was not long before he was spotted by a guard who raised the alarm.

For trying to escape he was given the biggest battering ever, it seemed to last for around fifteen minutes. Larry often wondered if this con had set him up to gain extra remission but he never saw the guy again, if he had he would have sorted him out. Larry was brought before the governor and for attempting to escape he lost some remission and was sent to Durham.

Durham had a reputation at the time as being the worst prison ever, a real primitive dirty place. If you get into trouble in Durham, you will really do take some stick. The governor having seen Larry's prison record and written reports about him singled him out as a bit of a rebel and therefore put him on special watch with stripes on his prison attire to signify so.

Larry remembers one officer in particular a real massive guy, probably around 20st. This officer confronted Larry

"Come here Rushton I believe you have been trouble during this sentence, well any aggro in here I will batter you so hard you won't be going anywhere else I will put you in a mental hospital".

This officer was not one to mess with, there would be no stepping out of line here and for once in his life Larry heeded the warning. Larry found out that this officer would take those to be executed to the executioner placing a hand on their shoulder he would guide them to their fate showing absolutely no emotion.

Larry now a marked man decided just to get on with it in Durham and finish off his sentence without causing any trouble, so it was back to sewing mailbags until he was discharged after 2 years.

CHAPTER 10

REVENGE – HELPING A FRIEND (EX-CON)

1960

So this time with only £4 in his pocket and the clothes on his back Larry headed back to Blackpool.

The girl he had been living with in Blackpool had moved on and thrown away all his gear so he had absolutely nothing really until a few pals had a whip round for him, enabling him to buy food and clothes. A guy called Gordon even sorted some transport out for him.

After a week of partying it was now time to get back to work. A pal of Larry's knew of a place out of town that looked as if it would be good prospect if they could get into the safe. Larry was immediately up for this, he said,

"Let's do it then"

This was the first job for 2 years so geared up and with false number plates on the car they drove to the property. On entering the premises, they found the safe which was old and relatively easy to open, a small explosion and the doors flew open. This was a better pay day than expected, so with cash in his pocket Larry visited a tailor he knew and treated himself to some new suits. Larry always dressed well, pristine in the most expensive suits available, his favourite being Italian made ones.

Whilst serving his last sentence Larry became good friends with Fred an inmate he viewed as being the real deal, a true professional in all fields, there was just something about him that spelt quality. Fred had been sentenced to 3 years for receiving stolen goods and was convinced he had been set up. Around this time it was rumoured that the police would have criminals working for them, fitting people up and lying in the witness box for them. Fred was sure this was the case because not long after he had received a haul of stolen goods there was a knock at the door, it was a police raid. One of the officers said to him

"We have reason to believe you are in possession of stolen goods"

Fred said nothing.

Most of the stolen goods were safely hidden away within the property so the police were only able to seize the jewellery Fred had on the desk in front of him.

Fred who lived in Leeds gave Larry his phone number so that he could get in touch when discharged from prison if he wished to. At this period in Larry's life all was going well, he was doing jobs right left and centre, had plenty of money, a nice apartment and would always turn out well dressed. An opportunity arose that Larry needed a really good locksmith for and he immediately thought of Fred. Fred was like the mafia he had plenty of pull and would be the ideal person to approach. Larry contacted Fred and then travelled to his home in Leeds, what a home it was magnificent, Fred had certainly done all right for himself.

As he approached the house Larry was greeted by Fred and then introduced to the family.

After a chat and few drinks Fred explained to Larry why he thought he had been set up, he was absolutely convinced this was the case when the police raid took place.

Fred leaned towards Larry as he was enjoying a single malt whisky and whispered to him

"Larry", "Are you up for some villainy, I know where the informant who set me up is and I want him hurt, break his legs"

"Oh and by the way I can sort out a locksmith for you"

Larry replied "Fred that will be no problem at all, cheers"

Fred provided Larry with a car, a place to stay and a photo of his target. Larry thought me may need some backup so he approached a pal of his to see if he would do him a favour and accompany him on this job. Larry knew his pal he could really look after himself and would be an ideal accomplice. A price for the job had not been discussed but Larry knew Fred wouldn't let them down. The plan on arriving at this guy's house was for Larry's pal to chin him as he opened the door then pin him down, Larry would then go on to break his legs.

Larry's pal looked at him and said

"Larry", "Are you going to break both of them"

Larry replied "I don't have to but if I am breaking one, I may as well break both"

The informant lived on the outskirts of town in a quiet area, the pair of them drove up to the property to find out he wasn't home, it was time for plan B they would just wait until he returned. They knew they could be in for a long wait as he was a bit of a jack the lad type of character, he enjoyed the nightlife and the drinking that went with it. After about 3 hours he arrived home, the pair of them hooded up moved in as he was parking his car, Larry's pal threw a punch but the informant was up for a fight so Larry stepped in too, hitting him on the shoulder with a bar and then went on to break both his legs. To make it look like a robbery Larry nicked his watch and the money he had on him.

With the job done Larry phoned Fred

"Fred, that's okay I have seen to that" not mentioning any specifics.

A week later Fred travelled over to Blackpool to meet up with Larry, thanked him for his help and then handed over four grand.

Larry said "no that's okay that was a favour"

Fred insisted Larry took the money as if it hadn't been for this informant Fred wouldn't have been charged and sentenced to 3 years in prison, this informant had it coming to him. Apparently the word on the street was that this informant had been working with the police for a long time and had set many criminals up who then went on to do time in prison. Larry was telling Fred the informant will probably put it down to a robbery I doubt he will be coming knocking at your door any time soon. Larry gave two grand to his pal who was well chuffed and then mentioned that he was meeting Fred the following week, so there may be some more work for him.

Larry travelled back over to Leeds where Fred took him out for dinner. Whilst dining Fred said

"Larry, I have another job for you if you are interested, but this is a little closer to home"

Fred's daughter had a boyfriend he and his wife didn't like but she was madly in love with him, somehow they wanted the relationship to end. The boyfriend was of mixed race and they didn't want any mixed blood in the family and were worried also that he may be into drugs. Fred and his wife had lost a lot of sleep over this boyfriend and they wanted to do something about it. The boyfriend was very good looking, Fred's idea was to maybe break his nose mess him up a bit then just maybe his daughter wouldn't be so in love with him and walk away, that was his hunch anyway. He also asked Larry to scare her boyfriend enough to make him want to leave town.

Having been fully briefed about the boyfriend, where he lived, his car, his movements Larry and his pal decided the best time to catch him would be late at night as he arrived back at his home, as they did with the police informant. Well the day arrived and the plan was to be the same as last time only this time it would be a broken nose. Larry's pal thought that to be a bit cruel, but that is what Fred wanted, that was the job. The arrangement with Fred was that he would ring Larry in a pub when the boyfriend had dropped his daughter off they would then wait outside his house awaiting his arrival. Well they waited for over an hour and he didn't turn up so Larry rang Fred to let him know. He was a bit of a night owl so maybe he was out clubbing.

Larry decided to call it a day they would wait for the weekend and try again on the Sunday.

Sunday arrived, Fred's daughter was at her boyfriends so the plan was to wait for him to drop her off back at her home, they would then follow him back to his own place. Eventually the pair of them arrived at Fred's house, it was a long wait around twenty minutes after he pulled up before Fred's daughter said goodnight and then got out of his car. As the boyfriend drove away they followed him expecting him to be returning home, but no he drove to a block of flats in quite a rough area. Larry was thinking this is as good an area to do him as any and its well away from his home. As they looked at the building there was a light on in the entrance hallway, Larry was thinking of doing him in the hallway as he was leaving so entered the property to scope it out, there was a lift so it was possible he may use that or walk down the stairs. Larry decided to go back to the car and wait, they must have been waiting around two hours when he then appeared at the door with a striking coloured girl in a dressing gown. Having seen that Larry decided to call of the assault, they would come back another time take a photo of him with the girl and then pass it on to Fred. Surely once the daughter saw the photo that would be the end of the relationship, job done.

Larry phoned Fred, explained the situation and convinced him that this was a better way of splitting them up. Fred was pleased, he knew that when his daughter saw the photo she would end the relationship immediately, which is exactly what she did. However, a week later Fred contacted Larry he still wanted the ex boyfriend harming, Larry questioned him as the end result had already been achieved but Fred was adamant he wanted him hurt so Larry and his pal carried out the request and roughed him up a bit nothing too bad no broken bones. Fred and his wife were extremely pleased with the outcome and in the years to come their daughter became a very successful business woman.

CHAPTER 11

MOVING BACK TO LONDON

1960

In 1960 there was not a lot going on in Blackpool so Larry decided that he would move back to London. He had enjoyed his time in Blackpool was out nearly every night and had earned plenty of money but he felt that at this time in his life moving back to London was the right thing to do. He mainly earned his living as a criminal, it was all he knew really and where better place to ply his trade than London.

On arriving in London he got in touch with a couple of pals of his Tony and Peter who lived in the Elephant & Castle area, they were well connected to the up and coming people including the Richardson's, so there were many opportunities for Larry to continue his life of crime. Larry had never carried a gun but on moving back to London he thought it was time he did. It was used on a few stick ups but more for show than anything else and to act as deterrent should anyone wish to have a go at him.

His lifestyle in 1960 was good really good he was out robbing during the day and then clubbing it at night without a care in the world. The pubs were certainly different in those days, the ones he frequented attracted a fine cliental, there were many aristocrats that he could mingle with and get to know, some really super people.

Larry eventually moved into an apartment in Bayswater and found it a superb place to live, there were many top restaurants just opening up at the time as well as many quality takeaways. The place had a really good vibe.

One evening whilst having a few drinks in a West End club with a friend of his Terry, Larry met a young lady.

Terry said "Larry that young lady at the end of the bar keeps looking over at you".

Larry replied "Terry" "she must be cross eyed or something then as there are a lot of good looking lads in here".

Maybe Larry was in with a chance he would always be smartly dressed, dressed to impress. Although his finances were good at the time if there was anything he needed, new suits, shoes, whatever, he used professional shoplifters whom he knew to lift them rather than paying. He would give the shoplifters a list of what he wanted, sizes etc. on some occasions he would simply point out to them the items he wanted and the shoplifters would do what they did best. It was much easier in the 60's too, security was nothing like today and no such thing as security tags. These shoplifters actually earned quite a good living they were not doing big jobs but what they did was on a daily basis so the money was always coming in. If they did get caught they would probably only be sentenced to three or four months and then they would be back in business.

Anyhow getting back to this young lady, Larry did like the look of her and he had nothing to lose so went over and offered to buy her a drink, which she duly accepted. After exchanging names (the young lady was called Rita), the pair chatted. Rita asked Larry where he was from and what he did for a living. Well he couldn't tell her the truth could he so Larry made out he was in the car game, and used to live in Blackpool, at least that bit was true.

Rita was trying to suss Larry out she said

"Larry I have heard of Blackpool, what's it like, you look like you have a few quid"

Larry replied "Rita It's not a bad place, seaside town with a lot of ordinary folk, not as sophisticated as here".

After many drinks Larry asked her if she would you like to come back to his for a drink, she turned him down but asked if they could meet up again in a couple of days.

Having agreed to meet, Larry turned up at the venue with his friend Terry. Time was getting on and there was no sign of Rita, Larry was checking his watch nearly every five minutes and just when he thought he had been stood up she emerged with a friend of hers. Having made introductions, the four of them sat down for a few drinks whilst listening to the cabaret. At closing time Larry and Rita went back to Larry's apartment where they chatted over a few more drinks. Rita told Larry she had a clerical job, as a typist, but as the night went on Larry having listened to her stories thought there is something not right here, her stories just don't add up. When Rita visited the bathroom Larry searched her bag but found nothing of importance just an old address book.

Rita came back from the bathroom and looking at Larry said,

"Can I ask you something, have you been in prison?"

“Yes” Larry replied

“What for” Rita asked

“Thieving, does that make any difference? “Larry replied.

Rita paused then said “No no difference at all, so you are not in the car game”

Larry replied

“I am when I can get hold of one (laughing), but basically I am a criminal”

A few days later Larry and Terry arranged to meet Rita and her friend again in a west end club for a few drinks and maybe dine out later on. After a few drinks Rita went to the ladies, but Larry became concerned as she had been gone for quite some time, he thought she may have left and gone back to her place near Euston. Rita finally reappeared.

Rita whispered

“Larry can we go now. I have been talking to some friends I am not keen on I really could do with leaving”

Larry replied

“But Rita I still have a couple of drinks here yet”

Rita again whispered to Larry

“Larry can we please go now, leave the drinks”

Larry downed the drinks he wasn't leaving them behind then said goodbye to his pal Terry and the pair of them left the club by the main entrance. They were just outside the club when a guy who was looking very agitated suddenly approached them shouting at Rita

"Give me my wallet back "

Rita replied "Wallet what wallet what are you talking about"

This guy becoming more and more agitated shouted again

"Give me my fucking wallet back you thief"

With all the commotion going on Terry came out of the club shouting

"What the fuck is going on"

When the guy saw Terry and his physique he backed off he was not someone you would want to get into a fight with. He continued backing away saying he would call the police. Without hesitation Larry moved forward hitting him on the chin, the guy hit the ground instantly there was no way he was getting back up, Larry then gave him a couple of kicks in the ribs whilst shouting to Rita.

"Rita let's get out of here, otherwise I will be arrested for assault or GBH"

The pair of them ran off and made their way back to Bayswater in a taxi.

Larry questioned Rita

"Rita what was that all about?"

Rita replied in a soft voice

"Larry I have a confession to make I am a pickpocket, I did take the wallet, took the money out and then threw the wallet away so if I was caught there would be no evidence"

Larry laughed he had always been suspicious of her being in a so called clerical job.

It turned out Rita's mother was a professional pickpocket, a very good one at that. Rita explained she was just carrying on the family business, she would work the pick pocketing three or four times a week, racing venues were always profitable as was the area around Harrods, the tubes not so good.

Rita asked Larry if he would be interested in helping her one day, she knew he could look after himself after seeing him down the guy at the bar. Takings would be split 50-50, Larry was quite happy to go along and see her in action so to speak.

Working as a team the planned approach was Rita would pick out a target and then give Larry the nod, Larry would then (1) Just follow her in case there were any problems, (2) Accidently bump into the target and Rita close by would move in (3) Act as a passerby, once the wallet was taken it would be quickly passed onto Larry, the pair would then meet up again at a pre-determined meeting place.

On one occasion Rita picked out a smartly dressed gentleman, red faced and stout in stature probably in his late 40s early 50s whom had just been shopping in a tobacconist. As he left the shop they followed him to a restaurant. Larry had a quick look through the window and could see he had a lot of money in his wallet when he took it out to pay for some drinks. The pair of them went into the restaurant so as to keep an eye on him and get a vibe as to when he may be leaving, this gentleman was enjoying himself and having finished off a carafe of wine was now sitting back enjoying a cigar. They didn't think it would be long now before he left so Larry and Rita settled their bill, left the premises and waited across the street for him to come out.

Larry said I may as well just knock him out then you can grab his wallet, but Rita was not up for this and wanted to follow her tried and tested method. As the guy left the restaurant Rita moved into action, walking towards him she stumbled and as the guy bent down to help her she dipped his inside jacket pocket. Larry watching from across the street couldn't believe what he was seeing she was good, very good. It was no wonder she enjoyed a really good life style, shopping in designer shops for clothes, shoes, handbags whilst dining out at some of the finest restaurants. This was a very good hit around a grand which once again was a great deal of money in the 60s.

Larry asked Rita if she ever checked wallets for addresses but she didn't she just took the money and ditched them. Larry was thinking a wallet containing addresses would be very useful, the home could be done at a later date, or the information could be sold on. This was something to be considered.

The pick-pocketing was going well but Larry had some sort of a sixth sense a strong feeling that someone was watching him, normally when Larry had these feelings he would step away but for some reason he ignored those feelings this time. After a good morning lifting wallets the pair of them decided to try and score a couple more hits in the afternoon so moved onto Oxford St. Rita spotted what looked like an ideal target and so moved in on the gentleman with Larry hanging back slightly in case it didn't go according to plan. Rita moved in front of the target and was going to feign a stumble expecting the target would help her up and then in that instance she would nick the wallet. However, before she had the chance suddenly two men ran towards her, at the same time another two were moving in on Larry he ran through back streets, shops and eventually got away. After a while Larry made his way to their designated meeting place but Rita never showed. He knew deep down she must have been nicked so returned to his apartment, with the belief that she wouldn't grass him up. Three days passed and there was no news so Larry visited her mother, he didn't know her well but needed to know what had happened. As he expected Rita had been arrested, apparently the police had been looking to nick her for a long long time. Larry wanted to visit Rita but her mother advised against it and to be honest it was a really bad idea. Time passed and eventually Rita appeared in court and was sentenced to twelve months. The evening paper that night reported the sentencing and referred to her as a professional pickpocket, Larry felt sick to the stomach he really liked her and wished he could have done something.

Towards the end of Rita's sentence Larry received a visiting order to visit her in Holloway, she now had only two more weeks to go before being released. During the visit she told Larry she was finished with the game and also told him something he wasn't expecting, she had a son who was being looked after by his father and on leaving Prison she intended to start a new life with them. Larry wished her all the best, saying that's a shame, I enjoyed working with you, you were a class act, he never saw her again.

CHAPTER 12

THE FIRM

1960

Larry was now doing a few robberies here and there with three sometimes four guys he knew but nothing major. At this time there were many blags going on which basically was a term used when getting a firm of criminals together to do a robbery. Larry became involved with one of these firms which was seven handed at times, one of the players happened to be a long distance lorry driver who used to drive up and down Europe advising on any potential targets. He would weigh up what loads were being transported mainly targeting loads that could be quickly moved on like spirits, cigarettes, food and clothes. If he was transporting a decent load himself, he would also just pull over and let the robbery take place then be given a black eye or cuts to make the robbery look authentic.

Another guy in the firm had a good fence in London who would buy and sell the crooked gear so it was soon moved on. Larry worked with this firm for some time as there were always jobs coming up some being better earners than others.

Whilst working with the firm Johnny an acquaintance of Larry's approached him about a jewellery robbery. Johnny knew a jeweller who regularly travelled to Hatton Garden with a boot full of jewellery for selling on to various jewellers' shops in the area, not only that Johnny knew the owner of a jewellery shop that this jeweller sold to. This jeweller he knew approached Johnny

"If you can rob the jeweller that sells to me I will buy the jewellery off you at a discounted price then we are both winners".

"Sounds good to me "replied Johnny"

The Jeweller said "The next time he visits me I will contact you then as he leaves you can follow him to see if he has an office or just deals from home."

The Jeweller good to his word contacted Johnny

"Johnny I am expecting a visit around 1 p.m. today but just follow him the robbery can't take place today. If the robbery is reported the police may retrace his steps and I certainly don't want them snooping around"

Larry and Johnny waited patiently outside the jewellers eventually the jeweller emerged with a minder by his side. They followed at a safe distance so as not to be noticed. He first of all stopped off at his office then proceeded on to his home.

About a fortnight later the day had come to stage the robbery, the jeweller would be doing his rounds that day and would be leaving his office loaded up with jewellery.

Larry asked Johnny what the plan was

"Are we just going to break in take care of the bodyguard then tie the jeweller up?"

Johnny replied "Yes we can do that I have got a couple of clubs we can take with us"

"Johnny there is no way I am doing this without having a piece with me"

"Well Larry if you are taking a piece I may as well take a sawn off shotgun"

"Okay Johnny you do that, let's get on with it"

The pair of them drove to his office, his car was there so he would definitely be inside and no doubt his minder would be close by too.

Larry said "Right Johnny lets storm the office"

Johnny replied "Ok let's do it Larry"

The door was surprisingly unlocked, so entry was easier than they both expected. As they entered the building they could immediately see the jeweller who was sat at his desk surrounded by boxes and paper work, the minder wasn't initially in sight but soon appeared and was rooting around for something, Larry was expecting him to pull out a blade but he actually pulled out a piece the two of them stared at each other.

Larry said "I hope you are going to fucking use that"

The bodyguard replied "Why is that"

"Well if you don't I am going to use mine"

The minder looked at Larry's gun and was now bricking it, taking a gun with him had saved the day.

Larry asked the minder to hand over his gun or use it, after thinking about the situation he handed it over, Larry was pleased how that played out as the last thing he wanted to do was pull the trigger. They tied them both up then proceeded to rob the place, no stone was unturned, this was going to be a big payday. Leaving the jeweller and minder tied up they fled the building. Larry then drove Johnny to the jeweller's shop to deliver the stolen goods in exchange for a few grand a good pay day for the two of them.

However, a few months later they heard on the grapevine that this jeweller had had them over paying nowhere near the worth of the stolen goods, there were some large stones taken that must have been worth a fortune on their own. Larry wasn't happy this had happened before to him so he asked Johnny

"What are you going to do about it?"

Johnny replied "We will just have to go into his shop hooded up and rob him"

They weren't going to tell him who they were and Larry was definitely not going to speak as his Lancashire accent would surely have given him away so it was agreed they would take a friend of Johnny's along Terry he would do the talking. The robbery was planned for a Saturday they knew the jeweller's routine, once the staff had left the jeweller would be on his own and go through his ritual of locking up and securing the shop. Saturday came it was time to rob the jeweller's. The three of them waited outside across the road from the shop. All was going to plan the

staff began to leave the premises, it was time to move. The three of them quickly stormed into the shop as the jeweller was about to lock the entrance door, they bundled him back into the shop and once inside the shop Terry gave him a crack to the head pole axing him, he then asked him for his keys, at no time did the jeweller realise who they were. Terry opened the safe where he found quite a sum of money and jewellery but no sign of the big stones they had expected to see. Having emptied the safe, they then took all the jewellery in the shop that was cased up. The jeweller was now sat in a corner scared to death, Larry kneeled down beside him and nicked his wallet which contained a good sum of money too. That was it payback time job done.
After a few more robberies Larry was once again feeling flushed with money and times were good. It was around this time in his life he started going to art galleries during the day as he had always been interested in art going back as far as his schooldays where he produced many quality drawings. He was learning all the time from the paintings and this stood him in good stead for when he started painting professionally later on in his life.

Still working with a firm the money coming in was decent but sometimes with as many as seven people on one job the money was probably not worth the risk of being caught. If Larry was caught he would be going down for a long time, he was waiting for one big hit then maybe he would go abroad but the waiting was a whole new ball game.

It's funny sometimes how things have a strange way of working out, the jeweller who had conned them and whom they then went on to rob got in touch with Johnny to see if he would be interested in doing some work for him. He was telling Johnny about the robbery that had taken place a few months ago, still no idea Johnny was involved and was wondering why some of the goods had not come back on the market. This jeweller thought he knew who had robbed him, another jeweller who had been in the game a long time. The work he had lined up for Johnny was to rob this jeweller expecting not only to steal his goods but also get back his stolen goods which he was convinced were in this jeweller's hands.

Larry asked Johnny to get the full low down on this Jeweller then they would rob him but not sell it to the jeweller who had conned them they would find another buyer. Having all the information they needed the robbery was on, but Larry had a chat with both Johnny and Terry he wasn't feeling comfortable something seemed wrong it was like he had a second sense or was physic. He didn't know why but it just didn't feel right then as luck would have it Terry was tipped off by his sister, her boyfriend told her that Terry needed to be careful the police knew he had been up to no good for some time and had been following him, Johnny and another guy who they didn't really know, presumably Larry.

The jeweller who conned them was apparently setting them up to be nicked. Even without doing the job now they could be charged with conspiracy, but that didn't really happen in those days. Terry told Larry that was it time to call it a day. Larry was dam sure it was, he was going to travel back to Blackpool now the police were onto them, they could get picked up for any job and it would be serious porridge, time to lay low.

The question was what to do about the Jeweller who set them up Larry thought about this.

"Guys we will leave it at least twelve months then maybe consider robbing him for a second time. Let's face it we have got away with one we have been lucky without the tip off we would all been doing time".

Larry returned to his flat packed up all his gear including his piece which he used to hide in the loft, and then headed for good old Blackpool once again. They never did return for a second robbery what was done was done and they had had a lucky escape.

CHAPTER 13

MANCHESTER HITMEN

Blackpool hadn't changed much since Larry had been away it was the same old people with the same old habits. Larry had been back in Blackpool just over a week when a pal he knew approached him to see if he was up for a job at an old mill in Accrington. Larry was up for it but wanted to check it out first so the pair of them drove up to the property, it wasn't going to be a problem a relatively easy robbery, so they decided they would return a couple of nights later and do the safe.

Having broken into the mill they found a large old safe in one of the offices. Larry had a root around before getting to work on the safe and found a cabinet well stocked with Champagne, Wine Whisky, Gin, and a few other spirits. Also in there was a wardrobe full of suit and shirts, on opening one of the drawers Larry pocketed a couple of gold watches and some cuff links he came across, then it was on to the safe. Larry wasn't sure if he would be able to blow both locks at the same time but on closer examination it looked as if the top lock hadn't been used at all, on the bottom lock there were scratches that had been made when the key was inserted, but nothing at all on the top one it looked brand new. Larry was sure they only had to blow the bottom one so it was back to the usual procedure, gelignite in the lock and then packing around the safe to deaden the noise, they used the suits and shirts from the wardrobe and a couple of rugs. Stepping well back from the safe they fired it up, a big explosion and it was open. The pair of them pulled a big iron box out of the safe and got to work on it with chisels, bingo there was a right few quid in it.

Larry carried on his thieving but was choosy now as to which jobs he took on. It was around this time in Blackpool that a few clubs were starting to open up for late night drinking, these clubs being more upmarket than the pubs and working men's clubs and were right up Larry's street. Larry was having a drink in one of these clubs one evening when he was approached by a guy who wanted to introduce him to Ken McGill an Irish doctor. After being introduced they sat down and had few drinks whilst they got to know each other. Larry gradually got on okay with him and over the years he became a very good friend in more ways than one. After knowing Larry for some time Ken asked him if he would like to do some driving for him as he had a foot injury. Larry thought about it for a while then thought why not, they enjoyed each other's company and used to have a good laugh together. Larry would ferry him up and down whilst he was visiting patients or hospitals. On one occasion he asked Larry to come into a boarding house with him rather than wait outside in the car. It was here that over a brew he was introduced to Ginger a patient of the doctor's. As Larry drank his cup of tea he knew straight away that Ginger was a crook, he was bringing all sorts of gear out for Ken to have a look at. It was then out of the corner of his eye Larry saw a young girl come in, she would be about eighteen or nineteen years of age, a stunning girl. Larry was sure she was giving him the eye but didn't like to say anything. As they left the boarding house Larry asked who the young girl was, she was Pat, Ginger's daughter.

Apparently Ginger had put a known villain up in the boarding house whilst he was on the run and his daughter having taken a shine to him was hanging around with him. Larry wondered if she would go out with him but didn't want to just walk in ask her, so he asked Ken if he would put a word in for him. Next time Larry saw Ken he asked if he had put a word in as yet, he had and said she would like to go out with him, but didn't want her dad to know as he was so possessive. Anyhow Pat met him at the end of the road the following day around 7.30 p.m., after a good chat Larry could see she was on edge and asked her what was wrong, she said her dad would not approve of her going out with a criminal. Well Larry wasn't going to tell him, he would never know. The two of them went for a meal, had a few drinks and generally had a good evening. Larry wanted to see her again on the following Saturday and told her to tell her dad she was staying with a friend. She couldn't do that though as her dad would check up on her, it wouldn't be good for her or Larry as he was well in with a Manchester mob. The pair of them did however meet up on the Saturday, went for a meal then onto a club in the south shore area of Blackpool well away from the north shore area where she lived with her father. Larry would see Pat most days now and it was whilst they were seeing each other that her father was arrested for dealing in stolen goods and given a twelve month prison sentence.

With Ginger serving his sentence not only did Larry and Pat have much more freedom so did her mother who was frightened to death of Ginger. Larry would often visit Pat's mother with her and was beginning to feel part of the family, during the week Larry would do a bit of business whilst Pat helped her mother out at the boarding house.

Larry continued to live in his Blackpool flat with only a few close friends knowing its whereabouts, he also rented a garage that no one knew about too where he kept most of his gear in case he needed to make a quick getaway. One day whilst in his flat the bell went so Larry went down the stairs to answer the door thinking it would be Pat or one of his friends, he was surprised to be confronted by a friend he used to pass stolen goods onto.

"Hi Larry how are you doing"

"Hi, how did you know where I lived who gave you my address?"

"I was playing cards in Manchester one evening when one of the players asked me if I knew Larry Rushton from Blackpool and where he lived"

"I told him I knew you but not where you lived as you were a person that kept yourself very much to yourself"

"This player then told me if I could track you down to let you know that Ginger had put a contract out on you and that you were going to receive a visit on the Sunday evening. Ginger has paid two grand to a couple of guys to give you a good going over or even do you in"

The player providing this information to Larry's friend detested Ginger and told him Larry needs to know what was going down. Larry knew straight away it was because he was seeing Ginger's daughter. Ginger was nearing the end of his sentence not long to go at all now so he obviously wanted this hit doing before he came out so the finger of suspicion would not be pointed at himself.

Larry's friend didn't know who they were but knew one was linked with the Manchester heavy guard and was supposed to be a bit tasty. Larry was now indebted to his friend and couldn't thank him enough he dug out a gold watch and told him to wear it as it was too hot to sell anyway.

Larry now pre warned needed to be ready for them, that evening he went over to see Pat, but not wanting to worry her he didn't mention what was going down, he just told her that he had to go away for about week on some business and was also going to turn his flat in as he was feeling uncomfortable with more and more people knowing where he lived. The pair of them went out for meal that evening and Larry told her he would keep in touch and see her soon. Larry then went to see a very good friend of his called Jim, told him about the aggro which was coming his way and he was in need of his help. Larry relayed the story and told him there would be a few quid in it for him but he refused to take anything Larry had done him favours in the past and now he was able to return the favour. Larry needed Jim's help to turn the situation full circle and take the hitmen by surprise

Larry went to see Jim on the Sunday afternoon so they could map out what they were going to do that evening. They would take them by surprise and in case they were carrying shooters or blades they too would also need to be tooled up. Larry was going to take a shooter and a baseball bat, Jim just a baseball bat. Jim was concerned that Larry was up for doing them in, but that was never on the agenda, he just wanted to send a message back to Manchester that the hit had failed and the guys took a bit of a pasting.

That evening Larry and Jim sat in a car with a good view on Larry's flat, not too close just far enough away so as not to be seen. The waiting seemed to go on forever and at one stage they both wondered whether the hitmen would actually turn up. Shortly after 10 p.m. a car pulled up and two really big guys got out of it, this had to be them. They rang the bell and on getting no response they got back into their car waiting for Larry to turn up. Things were falling into place nicely.

Larry said to Jim

"Right let's go and do them and here is a blade just as a precautionary measure, if they are looking to kill you use the blade and if you are not up for that walk away now and I will take them on myself".

Jim was ready he wasn't going to let his good friend down. They both got out of the car and approached the hitmen's car, Larry tapped on the offside front side window, as the window opened Larry glared at the driver and asked him if he was looking for Larry Rushton, they looked slightly stunned and worried at the same time, as the driver went to open his door Larry took out his gun and fired two shots over the driver's shoulder into the back seat of the car so as not hit them. The both of them were now bricking it, they asked what was going on but they both knew this had to be Larry Rushton.

Larry with a grin on his face said

“What’s going on is that you have found your target I am here standing right in front of you, get out of the car and walk over to the alley you can see behind me if either of you make a move I am going to do you both in”.

Holding a gun to the biggest guy’s head he told Jim to tie them up, both of them were now looking really scared and claimed that they only came over to talk to him. The tables had been turned, with them now both tied up Larry and Jim walked them further back into the darkest area of the alley and told them to get back against the wall and kneel down in front of it.

The two hitmen were now pleading for mercy

“Ginger asked us to pay you a visit and gave us two grand to do so. Jim searched them and found about £400 there was nothing else of any other value on them the watches they wore cheap imitations.

By this time these two guys were shaking,

Larry spoke

“I am going turn you back to Manchester and you can tell everyone you ran into me tonight and if I ever see you again and I will do you in”

Larry then hit the biggest guy across the head with a baseball bat and followed up with a couple of cracks to the ribs, that was him sorted, he then turned towards the other guy who was knelt down, he broke his ankle then also gave him a whack to the head.

Larry stared at them saying

"If you ever fancy another shot at me you had better come more prepared"

"Go back to Ginger and tell him the next time I see him I will put one straight through his head".

Years afterwards Larry was talking to an acquaintance of his who told him that these two hitmen had been boasting on their return to Manchester that they had been to Blackpool and sorted Larry Rushton out for seeing Ginger's daughter.

Larry never got to tell Ginger the true story, he did see him once more but didn't get the right opportunity to confront him.

CHAPTER 14

GLASGOW

With all that had gone down in Blackpool Larry thought it best to leave the town in case any other idiots came looking for him, so he decided to head for Glasgow and catch up with an old pal of his Neil. The pair of them did some thieving here and there making a few quid along the way but again nothing major.

On one occasion Neil was telling Larry about a farmer he knew that may provide them with a good payday. The farmer once a week on a Thursday would routinely make up his staff's pay packets at home for handing out the following day. Larry thought this sounded like a good opportunity.

Larry said "Neil, well it's Thursday today let's drive to the property and assess the situation"

As luck would have it when they arrived at the property they could see the farmer in his office with bundles of cash making up the wage packets.

Larry said to Neil "No time like the present we are here now so let's rob him "

Neil wasn't really feeling prepared and was also feeling a little anxious, but knowing Larry he knew it was going to happen one way or another Larry was not one for letting an opportunity escape him so he asked Larry what the plan was.

Larry's plan couldn't have been more simple, he would simply just break in through the office window.

"Okay Neil let's do this you drive the car down the lane and around the corner and give me your coat" said Larry.

Neil replied "Why do you need my coat"

Larry responded "I am going to put it over my head, jump through the window and grab the money"

Neil thought this to be a bit risky but went along with the plan and moved the car, engine running ready for a quick getaway.

Larry sneaked his way up to the window, the farmer was now right in front of him with the bundles of cash. Larry wondered if there might be anyone else in the house but there were no obvious signs of anyone being present.

There was no backing out now he jumped through the window landing directly in front of the farmer who just looked at Larry wondering what the hell was going on as he turned white as a sheet

Larry spoke "I am here for the money and have no intention of hurting you"

Larry gathered all the money together stuffed it into some bags that were close by and made his way back to the window he had just broken through. As he was making his way out the window the farmer took a flying leap launching himself at Larry, the pair of them were now hanging half way out of the window the farmer had Larry by the neck and had no intention of letting go he was up for a fight, however Larry eventually managed to wrestle himself free and was off down the lane cash in hand.

Moving to Glasgow turned out well for Larry he was having a good time and also a very profitable one to boot. Whilst out shopping one day he called in at a gentleman's outfitters to purchase shirts, it was here he met a shop assistant called Jean whom he got chatting with, having bought the shirts she asked him if he needed anyone to wash and iron his shirts as she offered this service to some of her best customers. Larry was well pleased and dropped his washing off on a regular basis. The more he saw of Jean the fonder he became of her and he eventually asked her to go out for dinner with him. Jean who was single at the time was more than happy to accept the invite.

Scotland was definitely a good hunting ground for Larry now he would do at bit of business then have the company of Jean to look forward to in his free time. The pair of them would dine out or just go for a few drinks or sometimes maybe both. Jean really took care of Larry and took him to some marvellous places and not only was she great company she was doing his laundry. The social life after being in London seemed strange to Larry, many people after a hard day's work would just go home, lights out at 9 p.m. to be ready for work the following day, this would be the time Larry was just getting ready to go out.

One evening after dinner out in a top Edinburgh restaurant the pair of them were driving back to Jean's when Larry noticed headlights behind him, for some reason he didn't feel comfortable maybe his second sense was kicking in again, all of a sudden he realised as the car edged ever closer that it was the old bill, he didn't say anything to Jean as she still thought he was a salesman a straight guy and that was the way he wanted to keep it. A little further down the road the police siren sounded, Larry wasn't hanging around and put his foot down in a brand new Ford Zephyr which a friend had nicked for him in Blackpool, he sped down country lanes not knowing where the hell he was going, the police pursuing them in what looked like a Wolseley.

By this time Jean was screaming wondering what the hell was going on

"Larry, Larry what are you doing, what do they want you for"

Larry replied "Speeding I can't stop because the licence I have is not mine and I will get in a lot of trouble"

Jean now acted as his guide directing him on the best way to go.

Having got away Jean questioned him "Are you telling me the truth"

Larry replied "Of course I am and I have no reason not too and apart from that I really like you"

"Larry I like you too and it would be nice to have something more permanent with you". She replied

Larry pausing for thought said "I do understand that but I do have to travel a lot and it would be much better if I could just see you when I am in Glasgow".

Jean was not feeling happy with that response

“I was hoping you would like to stay with me”

Larry told her “I can’t there is not enough work for me here at the moment just bits and pieces now and again”.

Jean never knew the truth about Larry being a professional criminal and that was the way he wanted to keep it. However, Jean did find out sometime later when Larry’s picture was shown in a national newspaper, headlining him as one of the most ten wanted men in England for robberies and other criminal acts. Jean couldn’t believe she was reading about the same person she never had a clue he was part of a criminal fraternity. The Larry she knew was always charming, smartly dressed, kind, and treated her well.

CHAPTER 15

BANK ROBBERY

1962

Having spent a fair amount of time in Scotland Larry was now back in Blackpool and it was not long before he was approached by a Londoner called Alfie, a very well dressed good looking young man but a person he regretted ever meeting as it proved unfortunate in so many ways. Alfie was now partnered up with Jimmy's widow Diane following his death at the wheel of his car. As Jimmy's death was not that long ago Larry was quite sure the pair of them may well have been having an affair whilst Jimmy was still alive.

Alfie was telling Larry about a bank in Yorkshire where if you were to walk down the main street you would literally see bundles of money piled up on a window ledge. Larry looked at Alfie in disbelief but let him continue talking.

"Larry the bank is on the second floor of a building, when you walk up the stairs you will come across the bank's entrance. On entering the bank you arrive in a reception area and then on looking beyond the reception you will see the stacks of notes all piled up. Larry you really need to come with me and take a look at this bank".

“Okay Alfie it’s worth me taking a look I will come with you, no point in wasting time we will go tomorrow“ Larry replied.

So the next day Alfie picked Larry up and they travelled to Yorkshire. Larry was excited at the prospect of robbing this bank but it all seemed too easy. Alfie parked the car a short distance away from the bank then pointed out to Larry the bank in question which was clearly visible. Larry and Alfie then made the short walk to the bank. On arriving at the building entrance Larry surveyed the area to get a clear view of its surroundings and to see if there would be any obstacles that may hinder an escape. He needed to retain a photographic image of the area in his mind. The two of them then entered the building and walked up a flight of stairs to where the entrance of the bank was. Larry opened the entrance door and once inside did a quick scan of the bank, this bank was not like the banks of today, it had a counter but there was no glass frontage, no cameras and true enough beyond this counter Larry could see stacks of cash piled up almost within reach, he could not believe his eyes, and was feeling a real buzz as this looked as if it would be an easy robbery. Shortly after entering the bank a bald headed middle aged gentleman approached them. Larry viewed him as a big fat greasy guy who had never done a proper day’s work in his life, behind him a clerk shaped like a milk bottle, probably in his 30s and then two women clerks. Larry had no second thoughts he had to rob this place no matter what happened it was just begging to be robbed.

Anyhow, Larry asked the gentleman who had approached him if he could open an account, which he intended to open in a false name. During their conversation Larry mentioned that he was looking to open the account with about four thousand pounds, the gentleman looked rather surprised but also delighted, even though Larry looked the part and was smartly dressed it was quite a sum of money in those days. They continued to talk both weighing each other up as they did so, then Alfie who was stood besides Larry began asking a few questions whilst Larry continued to weigh up the bank, the counter to the window where all the money was stacked up would have been no more than twenty yards away. This bank didn't feel right to Larry he had never seen one like this before, the money in full view not tucked away in draws or safes, it looked as if they were packaging the money up to be shipped out. Larry told the bald headed gentleman that he wouldn't be opening an account that day but he would be back to do so. Too true he would be back.

After leaving the bank Larry and Alfie surveyed the surrounding area for a second time, the bank was smack in the middle of town but there was there an ideal spot to park a getaway car in an alley just further down the road. The pair of them then evaluated how long it would take for them to reach the main roads, a mere five to ten minutes. Larry was well pleased they could do the bank and be out of town in no time whatsoever. Larry told Alfie we will return next week on the same day, same time mid-afternoon which was near enough the banks closing time and case the joint for a second time, hopefully the bank would be carrying out the same routine. In fact, Larry decided it would be better to turn up an hour earlier and look at the number of customers going in and out or indeed if there were no customers inside at a particular time. It would be too risky hitting the place if it was full of customers.

The following week the pair of them arrived on the same day but an hour earlier, true enough it was the same routine. Having now sized the bank up twice they decided to return the following week and carry out the robbery just before closing time. Larry told Alfie he would get hold of a plated car and then catch up with him during the week to finalise the details. As agreed the two of them met up and discussed the plan over a few drinks. There would most likely just be the four people in the bank; the big fat guy, the skinny guy and the two women, Larry would vault over the counter steam into the fat guy, give him a couple of cracks with his cosh, the skinny guy seeing this would probably lose his bottle and do nothing, but if he did Larry would also give him a crack Larry's only concern was the women screaming or setting an alarm off. Whilst Larry was taking care of the two guys Alfie would be right behind him with a bag gathering all the money together, that was all he had to do. An alternative plan was to take a handgun, stick the gun to the fat guys head and march him to the counter, telling them all to keep quiet whilst Alfie gathered the money together.

Alfie wasn't keen on using firearms in case something went wrong, Larry pointed out that in this game anything can go wrong firearm or not so he had better decide which option he preferred, Alfie was far happier with the first option and no firearms.

The day for the robbery arrived there would be no turning back now. Larry in a plated car arrived at Alfie's and asked him if he would drive. Larry could see the excitement in Alfie as they made their journey to Yorkshire but he also sensed somewhat anxiety in him. Larry was excited too and experiencing a tingling sensation in anticipation of the robbery.

Larry wanted to calm Alfie down and said to him

"Alfie just think of this as going into a fight, we are in a pub and we are going to kick our way out, it's as easy as that in fact probably easier the two guys have probably never had a fight in their lives, there is nothing to worry about".

Although the staff in the bank had seen Larry a couple of weeks earlier he assumed they would not recognise him as he was not from Yorkshire, if he went in with a mask he probably wouldn't get anywhere so he had to put his face on show slightly covered up and take a chance.

On arrival they parked the car in what they thought would be a good getaway spot, in those days parking was never a problem there were no meters, traffic wardens or cameras to worry about. Larry then went through the plan again with Alfie to make sure he knew how the robbery was going to unfold.

"Once I take out the fat guy and jump over the counter all you have to do is follow me and load the cash into your bag, don't concern yourself with anything else and once your bag is full give me a nod and we will be off"

Alfie who was now sweating profusely replied

"Right Larry right okay"

The pair of them made their way up the stairs towards the bank and lo and behold as they entered the bank the fat gentleman with his big pudding face was in the reception area

"Good afternoon what can I do for you"

Larry replied

"I was in here the other week regarding the opening of an account"

"Oh err err yes I think I do remember"

Larry gave him some name and then glaring at him said

"Today I will be making a withdrawal"

The guy replied

"What are you taking about, what do you mean"

Within a second Larry hit him, this was a shock tactic that really worked the gentleman looked at Larry with his mouth wide open, Larry followed up with another blow right on the side of his nose blood splattered everywhere, he was now lying on the ground whimpering like a big hound, making sounds like a dog. As this was happening the other guy jumped up from his desk, stuttering whilst walking over, Larry gave him a dig to the ribs and then used his cosh catching him on the side of his head, both men were now lying down on the floor with the two women just looking on. Larry turned around expecting Alfie to be grabbing the money but there was no Alfie he couldn't believe it Alfie had legged it done a runner on him. Larry was fuming, why would he do a runner. Larry had to act quickly now but with no bag to collect the money in he had to improvise so he opened his shirt at the front and started to stuff bundles of notes into it, in the meantime one woman started screaming and one of the guys was trying to get up off the floor shouting

"You've robbed us you've robbed us".

Larry was now thinking to himself what a pantomime this is and with as much money as he could gather he was out of there. As he was running away he noticed the skinny guy was in pursuit, Larry continued to make his way to where they had left the car, no car Alfie had taken it. Larry was raging now and as he was thinking what next the skinny man was at the end of the alley shouting

"He has robbed the bank; he has robbed the bank".

Larry put his hand into his inside pocket telling this man.

"I have got a gun and if you don't move out of the way, I will blow your fucking head off"

The man went as white as a sheet and stepped aside as Larry brushed past him running down street after street before jumping onto a bus with the bundles of notes stuffed into his shirt. Larry bought a ticket with the loose change he had in his pocket and then having travelled for some time got off the bus by a cinema, maybe this was a lucky break he went into the cinema and remained there for about three hours, hoping the search for him would quieten down. As Larry sat in the cinema he was thinking "This is charming, what am I going to do now" by chance he had a phone number of a pal of his who lived near Goldthorpe, in Yorkshire. Larry had used this pal of his a couple of times before and was sure he would help him out so he found a phone box and gave him a call,

"Hi it's Larry I am in a spot of bother can you meet up with me as soon as possible"

He told Larry to stay put stay where he was he would pick him up in about 25 minutes in a green Austin, well he did but it was more like an hour which seemed like an eternity to Larry. This pal then asked Larry

"What's up Larry, what's the score"

"I have just got myself into a bit of bother. Is there any chance you could drive me to Blackpool for a few quid?"

What had taken place was never mentioned.

His pal duly obliged, Larry now back in Blackpool was feeling exhausted and drained his thoughts not good ones turned to Alfie. The following morning there was a knock at Larry's door and who should be stood there but Diane.

Diane said "I have heard about your trouble"

Larry replied "What trouble I haven't got any trouble what are you talking about"

Diane said "Alfie has told me what happened and if you do anything drastic to him I think he will go to the police

Larry replied

"Let's get this straight Diane if I do anything drastic to him you will go to the police because I know what you are like"

Diane replied

"Well I don't want him hurt, hurt in anyway whatsoever. He lost control panicked and even wet himself"

Larry was not at all impressed

"Diane you told me this guy was one of the chaps he could do the business. Alfie is a real weakling, how he pleases you I don't' know, but apart from that I don't rate you anyway, I have never rated you, Jimmy was wasting his time with you. I know your calibre and I am going to tell you something Diane if you drop me in it, I will do you, no doubt about that"

Diane nervously replied

"I am not going to do that"

Larry was thinking well this will save the day for the time being I will deal with Alfie later.

Larry left it for a while then decided to do nothing about it, he wanted to but was frightened he would drop himself in it. As it happened Larry was out one evening when he ran into Alfie, he got hold of him

"You are a fucking bastard you are"

Alfie responded

"Larry I couldn't control myself, I was shaking that bad I thought I was going to feint I had to run out"

Larry not amused

"Is that why you took the fucking car and left me. What kind of a guy would you be if we were in the war? together, if I got shot you would leave me there, what a fucking dog you are, you had better look over your shoulder every time you go out".

Alfie looking scared

"I am sorry Larry really sorry I feel so ashamed"

Larry responded

"All that mouth you had about being a gangster, battering people, what you could do to people, what you have done to people, those you robbed in London and that all your pals were top fellas. In one way you have done me a favour,

I have learnt a valuable lesson I will never take people on trust again unless I have the full SP on them.

Between the bank chaos and Alfie (the so called big London gangster) Larry always had it in his mind that this is one mistake that may come back to haunt him. Alfie and Diane preyed on his mind so much so that he did consider doing both of them in, he couldn't do one without the other though as the finger would be pointing in only one direction. However, after serious consideration Larry decided he couldn't, he had never taken a life before and he wasn't about to start now it was not a road he ever wanted to go down.

Taking Alfie and Diane out was never going to happen but Larry always felt that in not doing so the robbery would get out and it would only be a matter of time before the police came knocking and sure enough they did, whilst out in Blackpool one day the police jumped him and arrested him for the bank robbery.

CHAPTER 16

LEEDS PRISON BREAK / ON THE RUN

1962 – 1963

Whilst awaiting trial Larry was remanded in Leeds prison for quite some time along with Alfie who had also been arrested. With Alfie also being arrested Larry had in the back of his mind that Diane had informed on both of them, he had no association with Alfie inside but felt strongly this would be the case. With Alfie pleading guilty and people recognising Larry he had no chance he was 'bang to rights' he had no chance of pleading not guilty.

Larry made many court appearances whilst on remand, the procedure always being the same, before being taken to court he would have to change out of his prison gear into the civilian clothes he was arrested in. These court appearances enabled Larry to become familiar with how Leeds prison operated, many prisoners would be brought into the reception area in the evening then the routine was: -

- Shower
- Fingerprints if they had not already been taken
- Change into prison clothes

The civilian clothes would be given to a trustee, (a red band as they were called) at a gate guarded by a prison officer, a real big slob of a guy who would just sit there drinking his tea. The gate he guarded was linked to the reception and also to a courtyard where the civilian clothes were stored in a type of warehouse. Having been through this clothes change over routine many times Larry thought he may have a chance of escaping as the prison officer always left the gate open so the trustee could switch the boxes of clothes over, the question was when did they lock that gate.

Larry got talking to an inmate who was going to be doing a lot of porridge and asked him if he was up for breaking out, having told him roughly his plan of escape this guy was not interested he thought Larry was off his head completely mad nobody had ever done it before.

Larry having spoken to a few other inmates was told the trustee stored the clothes either civilian or prison on racks in the storage area, these racks maybe as tall as fifteen feet, to reach that high there has to be a ladder. Larry once again asked the inmate looking at a long sentence if he was up for it.

"No Larry not for me but out of interest how exactly do you think you are going to escape"

"I am going over the wall, I will take the ladder in the storage area to climb above the reception, from there I can climb up and onto the side of another building and once on the top of the building lift the ladder up and take it with me".

The inmate still thought he was crazy, he would never be able to pull that off. Larry wasn't concerned in the slightest he had nothing to lose really, he knew he had a lot of time coming and the worst that could happen would be to lose some remission and take a battering, for a chance of freedom, he was sure it was worth the risk.

This inmate then told Larry

"You know what maybe I will come with you"

"Don't think for too long as I am not hanging around". Replied Larry

The inmate in the end decided to back out, he didn't have the nerve to try the escape and wished Larry the best of luck. Larry had been hoping he would be up for it as he could have done with his help and didn't trust anyone else.
The day arrived when Larry was going to go for it, he had just been sentenced in court to 5 years and was taken from court back to Leeds prison. On arriving back at the prison that evening he took his civilian clothes off put them into the box provided and then changed back into his prison gear which had a yellow stripe down both the leg and jacket as he was on special watch, he then sat down in the reception area waiting to be taken to one of the prison wings. Prison officers were now starting to enter the reception area calling out names of prisoners and the wings they were to be taken to. Larry now knew he only had a small window of opportunity to attempt the escape and told his acquaintance that had backed out that this was it he was going for it, the inmate again wished Larry the best of luck. Larry responded by telling him if you hear a big commotion going on and lot of shouting it is odds on I have been captured.

So it was now or never, a prison officer was guarding an open gate about 30 yards away from where Larry was sitting. It was this gate that led to the storage area, never in his wildest dreams would this officer be imagining what was about to unfold. Larry was now feeling excited at the thought of escaping he was really up for it, as the officer guarding the gate was shouting out instructions Larry somehow sneaked past him doing a left and then a right, in the darkness of the prison he could see in front of him a light above the open gate that led to the clothes store room. Larry entered the store room where he came across a trustee who was responsible for switching over civilian clothes to prison ones and vice versa.

This trustee looked at Larry

"What do you want"

Larry responded

"I have come for my fucking clothes"

The trustee responded

"What do you mean you have come for your clothes"

With that in a split second Larry caught him with a punch to the nose whilst telling him he was after the ladder, there was no response from the trustee he just stood there and said nothing much to Larry's amazement, why was he not calling for assistance. Larry now had the ladder which he leant against a wall followed by another wall that led him to a roof over the reception area, from here through the dirty skylights he could see the inmates sat down below and the prison officers walking up and down. All this time Larry was expecting it to kick off surely the trustee would by now have raised an alarm. From the reception roof Larry made his way onto the top of another building heading towards a major wall. On reaching the wall Larry leant the ladder up against it his freedom now within touching distance, from the ladder he was just able to touch the top of the wall and pull himself up. Looking down from the top of the wall he could see nothing the area was in complete darkness all he could do was drop down and hope for the best. On landing he damaged his ankle, it was not broken but badly strained all he could do now was hobble away as best he could knowing time was of the essence.

Although in pain he felt marvellous he had cracked the freedom trip, the feeling was as if he had just won a few million. Larry continued to hobble his way down the cobbled streets and alleyways, moving ever further away from the prison he then crept into someone's back yard where he found a shed door open, this would be a good place to collect his thoughts whilst also taking a much needed rest. He desperately needed to cover up his prison clothes and was hoping he may find a backdoor open where maybe the residents hung up their coats. Larry went from one backyard to another and as luck would have it on reaching the third one he saw some coats and overalls hung up in a back porch way that was lit up, this was his chance the door was open slightly so he crept in taking the overalls and a heavy coat. He was now able to cover up the yellow prison stripes and lose his zebra image, a little further down he found a bike. Keeping away from main roads he cycled away continuing to distance himself from the prison and the sirens that were ringing out.

After a while Larry stumbled across a building which appeared to be empty, he cracked a window open climbed in and took a look around, as he made his way past stacks of cardboard boxes as luck would have it he spotted a phone, this was great news he could now make a few phone calls. By this time Larry was feeling extremely excited but also exhausted and realised that he was now well and truly wanted, there would be man hunt on for him, he would have to escape the area the best way he could so he phoned a friend of his George who on answering the phone asked who it was, Larry replied

"It's me Larry"

George was puzzled

"Are you ringing from the nick Larry"

Larry responded

"No I am out of the fucking nick"

Again George was rather puzzled

"You have to be joking you have only just been sentenced today a friend of mine told me you got 5 years"

Larry laughing

"I did but escaped before they banged me in a cell"

His friend was still not having it

"You are pulling my leg aren't you"

Larry confirmed

"No I am out, I am free, I have cracked it"

George was still not having it he couldn't believe it.
Larry said

"You had better believe it as I could do with your help, can you pick me up, and by the way I could do with some money I don't have a penny to my name I must get out of Leeds".

George said

"Of course Larry where do want picking up?"

Larry found the address of the building he was in on some office paper work so he was able to give George the exact location. George took the office phone number Larry was ringing from and arranged to call from a phone box when he was close by. Approximately 2 hours later George picked Larry up.

"This is unreal Larry you are all over the news and now you are sat beside me, this is just unbelievable". "How did you get on in court?"

Larry replied

"It wasn't too bad I used a bit of philosophy I knew I was going to get porridge, so after talking to my brief I put all the blame on my shoulders telling the court I had led Alfie on and he wasn't really a crook, this was all down to myself"

His brief was right the sentence was less than it could have been. The judge in sentencing Larry told him a few people had spoken very well of him so obviously he was not all that bad and in carrying out the robbery he could have really hurt the staff, especially had he gone in with a gun. This robbery also appeared to the judge as more of a spur of the moment opportunity, a chance was taken. The judge in looking at Larry's history and past offences believed he had never been given a real chance in life and whilst gazing at Larry told him he was going to give him a chance, he felt that he must have some good in him so instead of what was looking like a 10 year sentence he would reduce it to just 5 years with a warning that if he didn't take this chance and appeared before him again he would be dealt with severely. The judge who had given Larry a chance went on to learn of his escape, he had escaped from prison four hours after sentencing. Larry's family on hearing he had been given 5 years and had escaped within four hours were completely gobsmacked. The newspapers were full of this incredible escape which may possibly be the quickest in British history. Larry was now part of a manhunt, newspapers reporting him as highly wanted and dangerous criminal.

- A jail's new man vanishes within 4 hours of sentencing.

- Late appeal to judge to give him a lenient sentence.

- Police cordoned off the area, circulating his description throughout west riding.

- Car squads swooped on all-night cafes and stopped late night travellers.

As George drove Larry out of Leeds he asked him what his immediate plans were, at this time Larry didn't really have a plan but was desperately in need of clothes. George told

Larry that wouldn't be a problem and that he would drive him to a friend's property not far away which was not currently occupied and there he could lay low for a couple of days, whilst he got him some gear together.

George was true to his word, he turned up with a top of the range car, clothes and some cash. Larry 's plan was to leave the area before he was spotted, his first destination being that of his elder brother Tom to tell him something, pick up some jewellery, personal gear and basically say "see you again". Larry was extremely grateful to George but he couldn't hang around he needed to get on his way.

The press was full of Larry's escape and he was also being connected to this that and the other, with his photo being well circulated he needed to keep his head down. Larry arrived at Tom's late one evening when it was dark. Tom opened the door totally surprised to see Larry standing there. Larry told him he had just come to collect a few things and was thinking Tom would want to help him out. The pair of them sat down and chatted whilst Tom's wife was making a brew. Tom was restless and on edge and eventually told Larry he should give himself up and that he couldn't stay with them as they would be harbouring a fugitive landing themselves in all sorts of trouble.

Larry just looked at him stared into his eyes in disbelief, thinking back to when they were kids living at home.

Larry stealing here there and everywhere. It was in those days that Tom would go through Larry's pockets of an evening whilst he was sleeping and nick most of the money, Larry never said anything. Now with his brother in front of him he felt nothing, he was now looking at a spineless, uncaring brother, certainly not a brother of his anymore.

Larry looking him straight in the eyes said

"Thanks a lot, I will always remember what you have just done ."

Larry was sure if he had stayed the night Tom would have turned him in for fear of being caught or for a reward, following that incident Larry never spoke to Tom again.

On that sour note Larry left to meet up with a pal of his, and to see if there were any jobs on the horizon, but there was nothing to be had so Larry made his way back to Burnley to meet a friend of his called Alan, he wasn't really a recognised face in Burnley anymore so felt relatively safe. Larry called at Alan's address knocked on the door to be welcomed in straight way.

Alan said

"Larry come on in it is great to see you, why don't you stay here for a few days while it all cools down"

Larry accepted the offer and was feeling reasonably relaxed considering he was a wanted criminal. One evening he stepped out to telephone some of his contacts from a local phone box, one of those being Neil whom he had worked with in Glasgow. Having spoken with Neil it was off to Glasgow he had some jobs lined up including safe breaking that Larry could assist with. On reaching Glasgow staying with Neil was an option but to due there past association probably not a wise move the police may well have Neil's home under surveillance so Larry decided to book himself into some nice digs where nobody knew him or would recognise him.

Whilst in Scotland Larry would definitely have contacted Arthur Thompson the notorious Scottish gangster and one of the most feared criminals in Scotland but at the time he was serving time in prison.

Larry and Neil soon got to work blowing a safe, the rewards of which kept them going, but Larry was becoming more and more interested in a possible robbery Neil had told him about when he had first arrived in Scotland. Neil's worry with this one though was the two big dogs the guy had protecting his home. Larry told Neil the dogs won't be a problem we will drug them, make them drowsy steak laced with cough medicine and whisky should do the trick if we leave it to soak into the meat overnight. Having surveyed the property it looked like a quick in and out job and then off down the main roads which were relatively close by. This target had made his money out of hijacking wagons full of goods and made plenty of money from it, he now spent most of his free time out on the lash with his wife, both of them big drinkers. Larry was thinking great this should be easy when they get home after a night out they will be both hammered and asleep in no time at all, we can then throw the meat over for the dogs and put them out of action.

Neil "Is there anything more I need to know about this guy"

"Well Larry he is a big guy, he can fight, he does have a bit of a reputation" replied Neil

"That won't be a problem Neil we will take him out first"

Neil continued

"So Larry how are we going to do it? are you up for a fight or do we stick a gun to his head"

"Let me have a think about that, first things first I wouldn't mind taking a look at him" responded Larry.

Neil told Larry he would be able to size the target up in his favourite pub, he would be in his usual spot propping the end of the bar up, a really big guy, very vocal impossible to miss. Larry could walk in and nobody would know him but they decided to wait outside so Neil could point him out. Having seen the man Larry was quite sure he wouldn't be a problem, the dogs were more of a concern.

On the night of the robbery the plan on breaking in was to tie this guy up giving themselves plenty of time to search the property. The pair of them waited for the man and his wife to return home, which they did, intoxicated as usual, the meat was then thrown over a wall to the dogs. It was now a waiting game eventually the laced meat seemed to have had the dogs over and with all the lights in the house out it was time to make a move. A stick was thrown over just to make sure the dogs were out of it, not a murmur so far the plan was working.

The pair of them broke into the property through a window relatively easily. They were in disguise gloved up carrying a knife, a hand gun that Neil owned and some gear to tie the guy up. The plan was to sneak upstairs and scare the man by placing a gun to his head and then tie him up, he would then be out of action and hopefully his wife would be unaware what was taking place. The two of them crept upstairs and eased open the door to the room in which the couple were sleeping.

Larry then put the gun to the man's head whispering

"Switch that light on"

The man opened his eyes

Larry whispered

"Keep fucking quiet or I will blow your head off"

The man half asleep unsure what was going on murmured a few words.

Larry continued

"Keep quiet we are going to tie you up"

He murmured a few more words and with that his wife woke up frightened to death, well anybody would be seeing two strangers in your house tooled up.

The man looked at his wife and said

"Don't do anything silly, just do as they say, don't do anything silly"

With that the couple were tied and up and gagged face down in the bed. The search for the safe was now on and found relatively easily behind some suitcases in a spare room. Larry was thinking this guy is probably a creature of habit and would always keep his key close by, he was right the key was in his jacket pocket attached to his car key ring. Result, there was plenty of money in the safe the robbery had gone well, the couple themselves had endured being tied up but apart from that and the emotional scars came out of the incident unharmed.

After that success and now with a tidy sum of money behind him Larry told Neil he would only be staying in Scotland for a little while longer to sort one or two things out then he was off abroad, probably to Spain and would see if Pat would accompany him. The problem was he could not show his face back in Blackpool he would be nicked for sure. Neil asked if there was anything he could do to help and he did so by contacting Bridgette a girlfriend of a man called John an extremely wealthy man who Larry knew very well. Bridgette was to be the go between she travelled to Blackpool to catch up with Pat and to explain the situation giving her a number where Larry may be reached. Pat called Larry she was going to leave home and travel to Spain with him, Larry therefore arranged for her to be taken from Blackpool to Bolton by taxi to meet up with Bridgette and John and from there she would contact Larry to make further arrangements.

The plan was for the two of them to meet at the Midland hotel in Morecambe a very grand and popular one in its day. Pat arrived at the hotel accompanied by Bridgette and John, she had taken a risk meeting Larry again but felt it was worth it. The four of them had an enjoyable meal together, Larry had already left the staff a few quid to look after them which they duly did, the food was excellent and the drinks were flowing.

Larry and Pat then left Morecambe in the early hours of the morning and headed for London where they were would be put up by a couple Larry knew, Arthur who he had served time with and his wife Sheila. Larry was telling Arthur of his plans for Spain especially as the papers were now reporting that he had kidnapped Pat, totally untrue of course but on top of his escape this story would sell papers. Spain was maybe a chance to start a new life and not waste another moment. As it turned out the Police on receiving a tip off turned up at the Midland hotel to arrest Larry, missing him by a mere 25 minutes, that was a close call.

The newspapers were full of the manhunt: -

- CID report man on run with his expensively dressed 18-year-old red haired girlfriend Pat Phelan may shoot. He may be armed with a sub-machine gun and an automatic pistol.

- Rushton still on the run 4 months after escaping from Armley prison, Leeds.

- Police officers warned to approach Rushton with caution.

- Police forces throughout Britain alerted to look out for a ford Zephyr with false number plates.

Larry now needed Arthur to help him out he was in need of a passport a driving licence and left handed car price would not be an issue. A few days later Arthur delivered the documents and a car which had been purchased from Wembley motors. Spain was now on, Arthur had hoped to travel over as well with his wife but couldn't make it so his wife and a friend accompanied Larry and Pat who had now dyed her hair black in case she was spotted. There were no problems reaching Spain, the journey was undertaken without incidence.

Larry should have been in a cell now but instead was enjoying life in the sun from an exclusive rented apartment in Alicante. The apartment was rented for six months cash up front, the couple he rented off assumed Larry had been left some money little did they know where his money came from.

It was now 1963 and Larry was finding it near impossible to spend his money, everything in Spain was so much cheaper around that time than in the UK. A night out dining and drinking plenty was costing about £6 for the two of them. It was like living in paradise. Larry had never experienced anything like it before, he would lie in bed of an evening thinking how lucky he was to be in Spain and not in a dirty stinking cell, his only care was keeping one step ahead of the law.

Larry was now splashing the cash, driving around in a top car and earning some sort of credibility. However, temptation was never far away in Larry's world he was not thinking big like banks but jewellers in particular were an attraction. It was not long before a friend of Larry's an expert in pick-pocketing and safe blowing visited him and it was whilst they were on a trip to Barcelona that they stumbled across a high class jewellers shop. In the jewellers was a ring that must have been worth a fortune but as it was the only one of its kind thieving it would be some challenge. Larry's friend Jack had an idea, he told Larry he may be able to have one made up to look very similar, if he could they may be able to do a switch without anyone noticing. Jack with his top connections was constantly hitting jewellers throughout Europe but it was around this time that channelling the goods into the UK was becoming rather risky. Jack was also convinced his movements were being monitored so the goods for the time being would have to remain in Spain, who better than Larry to hang onto the gear which is exactly what happened. Eventually the goods were moved on with Larry being paid handsomely for looking after them, not only was he paid well but Jack gave him a gold bracelet and a ring which nowadays would probably fetch around 40K. Larry soon moved this ring on though he couldn't risk being caught with it, if he was he would more than likely be held responsible for the robbery and a significant prison sentence that would have followed. One day whilst Jack was over he Larry and Pat where out driving when they stopped in a town where they found a church located at the top of a hill people climbing up to do their worshipping. So whilst there all three of them thought they may as well take a look around the church.

Jack turned to Larry

"You are not going to believe this look at the Madonna with all those big rings on her fingers"

Larry replied

"They will just be pieces of glass"

"No Larry that's what they will want people to think, with a trained eye I can tell you those are uncut diamonds"

"No way, not a chance" replied Larry

Jack continued

"Larry I am telling you they are for real as are the pearls and sapphires"

Larry smiled at Jack saying

"Jack, well that's it I am back here tonight"

However, Pat found out what Larry was intending to do and went mad telling him in no uncertain terms if he did she was off and would have nothing more to do with him. Larry for once backed away from the opportunity he didn't think Pat would grass on him but if she left him who knows what might happen and the pressure that might be put on her under an interrogation. He was also still not convinced the gems were real, how could they be?

Whilst in Spain Larry and Pat became friendly with a Spanish couple who owned a riding stable about 500 yards away from their apartment. One evening they met this couple in a bar which again was very close to their apartment just across the road and down a street. As they were enjoying a few drinks the couple invited Larry and Pat to the stable for horse riding lessons, neither Larry nor Pat had really been close to a horse let alone ride one but they accepted the invitation. After a few lessons they would arrange to pick up a couple of horses and then ride them down to the beach where they would catch the rays of the sun whilst enjoying a picnic. After taking the horses out on many occasions Larry and Pat were becoming really good friends with this Spanish couple and were cordially invited to a party they were hosting one evening. It was during this party Larry was introduced to a local liqueur, well this must have been extremely strong as it had both Larry and Pat over they slept all the next day and most of the evening too finally awakening to find themselves in a guest room with little recollection of the previous evening. Larry at once checked his back pocket his money was still there so that was a bonus. Apparently they had a good time drinking and dancing the night away until they became too tired and were offered a room. Larry learnt a lesson it was the worst he had ever been on alcohol he had never passed out before and making himself so vulnerable through drink was something he never wished to repeat, having a good drink was one thing but not to the point where you may not be in control of a given situation.

Larry was continuing to have a wonderful time in Spain, enjoying the sunshine, driving here there and everywhere to discover new places, it was paradise and freedom, something he did not want to end. However, in life all good things come to an end eventually and this episode in his life was just about to do exactly that as you were only allowed to reside in the country for a few months.

Larry became known to the local police who knew him as Al Palocci, they would look on him with envy he seemed to have everything, a top apartment, a great car a lovely girlfriend and money to burn. Anyway the time was drawing near that he would have to return to the UK, he didn't want to get pulled by the police for outstaying the permitted time and for them to maybe then take a closer look at him to find out he was really Larry Rushton. So returning to the UK it had to be, besides anything else money was beginning to run out from all the partying and having such a good time. Larry made contact again with his safe blowing accomplice Neil to see if there was any work lined up that he could become involved with, there was so he asked Neil to find somewhere nice for him to stay in Edinburgh and told him he would be back in a week's time. At the time Larry was returning to the UK the great train robbery had taken place and security was tightened. Driving back in his American car Larry was stopped by customs and asked to drive to a holding area where the car was then searched extensively, taking the car apart as they did so. Larry and Pat were both questioned under their assumed names, this was now a tricky situation Larry's bottle was beginning to waiver but he remained calm, would they recognise him as the wanted criminal he was, luckily customs found nothing apologised for the inconvenience and that was it the pair of them drove away and made their way to London where Larry immediately traded his car in for a small ford.

Whilst in London Larry met up with a couple of his pals and then it was off to Edinburgh to meet up with Neil who had sorted out an apartment for them. Settling back down in the UK was not so easy after their few months in Spain the weather in particular was a real downer, Larry was also now on edge although in disguise with a hair piece he felt it would only be a matter of time before he was spotted and turned in.

With money dwindling away it was time to get back into business Neil discussed with Larry a jeweller's he had lined up, Larry took a look at the place, it was ideal and this would be a big score but they really needed a driver. Larry and Neil would do the business whilst a getaway driver would wait outside. Larry knew a driver from London whom he could trust so until he was available the robbery would have to be put on hold. Whilst waiting for the driver Larry kept a low profile but still dined out and socialised in some of the pubs. There was one particular pub in Glasgow Neil wanted Larry to accompany him too, it wasn't really Larry's cup of tea but he went along as he wanted to meet a guy in there, unfortunately this guy wasn't there. Whilst there Larry got chatting to Rubin the owner who recognised Larry instantly, he had been introduced to him in the past.
Rubin commented

"I know you, you are Larry Rushton, aren't you on the run?"

Larry replied

"No you must have got that wrong, not me you must have got that wrong"

Rubin continued

"Are you sure I read about you in the papers"

Larry again replied

"No it's not me" then left it at that.

As it happened Larry had to return to this pub one night for a meeting it was around the time Kennedy was assassinated as it was a real talking point everyone was talking about it. Larry told Pat he would see her later and set off for Glasgow.

Larry arrived at the pub and the first person he saw was Rubin who asked Larry what he would like to drink. Larry was chatting to Rubin when he saw out of the corner of his eye two men making their way towards him and on looking through the bar towards the other side of the pub he saw another two men blocking the doorway. Larry knew instantly that was it he was going to be nicked.

The men approached Larry and pinned his arms to his sides, having Larry in their grasp they said

"Larry Rushton"

"No who's that I am not Larry Rushton I am Al Policci"

The police continued

"Well we believe you are Larry Rushton, we have photos of you and you are now under arrest"

Larry just choked someone had turned him in, nobody knew he was going there so he had no idea who it was and he never did find out. He thought maybe Rubin but didn't really believe it would have been him.

Larry was taken to the police station where he was stripped of his clothes then questioned.

"Larry Rushton you are going to be held at Barlinnie prison on remand for a day before we transport you back to Leeds prison"

Larry was sitting in his cell thinking about his return to Leeds not something he was looking forward to when suddenly his cell door opened he had a visitor it was Arthur.

"Larry sorry to see you have been nicked, is there anything you need any messages, what can I do for you"

"Arthur when would you be able to get a message back to me" replied Larry

"Probably tomorrow" Arthur said

"It's too late Arthur they are transferring me back to Leeds tomorrow" Larry replied.

Arthur looking at Larry said

"Fucking hell I wouldn't fancy that Larry"

"No I don't either" replied Larry

"So is there anything you need" replied Arthur

Laughing as he said it Larry said

" A hacksaw"

Arthur busted out laughing too "you are a cheeky bastard you have just been locked up again. If I can do anything for you now or in the future, you only have to ask"

By this time Larry had also been informed that Pat had been arrested.

In the morning a police escort arrived to transfer Larry back to Leeds. As he was leaving through the gates he ducked his head as the press took photos to support the stories they would write about his escape and capture. On his way back to Leeds he was thinking they are really going to make a meal out of this, he would be in for a real rough time not least from prison guard colleagues that had worked with the two officers that had been dismissed following the escape.

On arriving at Leeds Larry was held in the reception area. An officer came over to him

"Ah Rushton you know this place very well don't you, get your clothes off, and let's have all that jewellery too"

Larry never said a word.

"We don't need a photo we have one from the last time you were in and we certainly don't need your fingerprints, so just put these prison clothes on and sit yourself down there, this officer besides you will look after you and take you down to the block, we are talking about the punishment block Rushton"

Larry wasn't surprised at all it is what he was expecting.

"Right come on now Rushton I will take you down".

Larry was thinking it all seems very quiet not many people about as he was marched along then taken through a door into a small wing leading to some cells. In the distance he could see all the screws lined up ready to steam into him.

The chief officer then spoke

"Oh you are Larry Rushton, you caused us a lot of trouble last time you were here by escaping and officers were in big trouble did you know that"

Larry responded

"No I didn't and I couldn't care less, I have not started my sentence yet so I can't lose any remission"

"You are in charge of this now aren't you well you need to know I have made a phone call and have a solicitor coming to see me tomorrow and the other thing you should know is that I underwent an examination in Barlinnie prison and I didn't have a mark on me, so you can please your fucking self, one way or the other what you want to do. If you do batter me, break bones, cause heavy bruising you as the senior officer in charge will be responsible and will lose your job I can promise you that"

The prison officer staring down at Larry commented

"Oh so you have sorted everything out have you"

Larry replied

"Yes I have incidentally, so you get on and do what you fucking have to do"

With that the officer slapped Larry across the face.

Larry looked at him "Is that it?"

The officer glaring at Larry responded

"It is for now Rushton take him down to his cell"

Larry was taken to his cell, everyone ignored him and left him alone not one person took a pop at him.

After some time inside Larry was brought before visiting magistrates.

"Right Rushton on such and such a date you escaped from this prison, what have you got to say for yourself"

Larry replied

"I don't have a lot to say for myself at all an opportunity was there it had always been there and I fancied taking it on. The greatest thing a guy can look for is freedom and you should know that I will escape again if I get a chance, so that's it"

The magistrate continued

"Do you have nothing else to say Rushton, sorry?"

Larry looking up to the magistrate replied

"Sorry!! I had the time of my life in Spain, living in paradise plenty of money I had a great life and now you are asking me if I am sorry, am I sorry am I fuck sorry"

The magistrate was not impressed

"You can cut out that language too Rushton off you go and if we see you again, you will lose any earned remission"

"Go fuck yourselves" replied Larry

"Right that's 10 days that will be lost for swearing at us, do you want some more"

Larry responded

"You can take the lot, I don't give a fuck and I will escape again the first chance I get"

The bottom line was six months earned remission would be taken away and there was no chance of another escape from Leeds as he was watched like a hawk.

Leeds had seen enough of Larry and Larry of Leeds it was now time for him to move on with a transfer to Dartmoor Prison.

CHAPTER 17

DARTMOOR PRISON

On arriving at Dartmoor Larry was brought before the governor.

"Well looking at your record you have hardly started your sentence as yet and you have already lost six months' remission you are not doing too well are you?"

"I guess not" replied Larry

The governor replied

"Well if you step out of line here you will lose all remission I can guarantee that. I will not have anyone escaping from my prison it has a reputation of being a good prison and a secure one. Why they have sent you here rather than keeping you up north where you belong I don't know"

Larry replied

"I guess they have probably sent me here as a way of punishment"

The governor responded

"Maybe so but whilst you are in my prison you will do as you are told"

Larry looking the governor straight in the eye

"Well I didn't want to come here if you want to transfer me back up north that's fine by me"

The governor asked his officers to take Larry away saying "You have a reputation Rushton no one has escaped on their first night in prison and I can assure you that won't happen here"

"Well that's it Rushton I don't want to see you again if I do you will be severely dealt with, now take him away."

Listening to all this Larry in the back of his mind was thinking how he would just love to give this governor a left hook.

Dartmoor was exactly what Larry thought it would be a very old prison a greyness about it that totally destroys you. Walking to the cells Larry imagined all the suffering that had taken place, this was a unique prison there was a stillness and quietness about it. Once in his cell Larry could hear nothing it felt more like being imprisoned in a tomb and made him think this is truly what a prison is all about. With Dartmoor being a fair distance to travel from the north Larry didn't expect to receive any visits not that he had any in previous prisons but he actually did his younger brother John whilst on his honeymoon paid him a visit. Larry was made up he really appreciated John taking time out to come and see him. John was asking Larry how he was getting on.

"John exactly as I expected really but I have noticed one thing I reckon I could escape from here"

"Larry don't start that again try to get your sentence done" replied John.

Larry continued

"John believe me the first chance I get I am going to go for it no matter what prison I am in"

"Larry just do your time then you are out" replied John

Larry looking across at his brother

"That's what I want but to be out sooner rather than later"

Dartmoor wasn't getting any better the place always seemed damp the walls soaked in moisture there was never a crispness about the place it was just a horrible. When Larry was taken to the exercise yard he looked on, everything about the place was grey, the walls, the prisoners all dressed in grey with their grey faces just walking around in a circle, a deadness about them, it was like something out of a horror movie.

As he was thinking this someone tapped him on the shoulder "Larry Rushton, I am Johnny"

Larry thought well that's a name from the past he was dating Pat prior to Larry whilst on the run in Blackpool. He had escaped from a train along with another inmate whilst being transferred from one prison to another.

Johnny asked Larry

"Is there anything I can do for you"

"Well not really unless you have some books" replied Larry.

Johnny patted Larry on the shoulder

"No problem Larry will sort that out for you"

Johnny was in part of the prison where the inmates had earned privileges and had more time out of their cells to sit around chat maybe play cards. Privileges was something Larry would have to earn but he had no intention of doing so, anyhow the two chatted whilst walking around the yard exchanging stories, Larry's escape from Leeds in particular.
For Larry whilst in Dartmoor it was once again back to sewing mailbags, a job he should have been an expert at by now but absolutely hated. However, whilst sewing the mail bags Larry made friends with Micky Cornwall, a Londoner who like Larry had always been a thief.

In the work room the prison officers would sit on big high stools so they could keep an eye on everybody and see what was going on. Talking was not really permitted but Larry and Micky chatted away as best they could and on one occasion Larry was having a bad day and told Micky that he was going to launch a pot of wax at one of the officers who had fallen half asleep to see if he could knock him off his chair, the wax about the size of a cricket ball was used for strengthening the sewing thread.

"Micky keep your head down" with that Larry through the wax but missed with the wax shattering as it hit the wall behind, however on the second attempt he hit the officer on the shoulder startling him.

"Who through that, come on whom through that?" shouted the officer.

Everybody just looked at each other, Larry and Micky struggling to keep their faces straight they found it hilarious and got away with it.

Micky looked at Larry

"Larry I thought you would have at least hit him on the head"

"I tried to let's have another go tomorrow, in fact Micky you have a go if you think you can do better" replied Larry.

The following day the same officer was on and warned the inmates that if yesterday's incident happened again the guilty party would be severely dealt with.

Larry nudged Micky

"Micky now's your chance he is nodding off"

With that Micky took aim and caught him right on the side of his face. After much laughter once again the officer had no idea who the culprit was. Larry and Micky thought they had got away with it but one of the red bands a trustee prisoner must have seen something and put Larry's name in the frame, because that evening Larry's cell door was opened.

"Right come on Rushton you are off to the punishment block"

"Why am I going to the punishment block, what for?" replied Larry.

"You know why Rushton, throwing wax at one of our officers" the officers replied.

With that Larry surrounded by four officers was taken down to the punishment block a real bleak place. Larry remembers it well because years later he featured this cell block in a painting he did whilst serving time. The painting which he sold and will still be around today was called "The Loser" a clown in the foreground with the cell block in the background.

Larry was back before the governor for the incident and received 14 days' solitary confinement and also lost another 14 days' remission, which was nothing new to Larry. Whilst doing solitary he expected a visit for some physical punishment but he never did get a visit and often wondered why not as this had always happened at previous prisons.

Larry happened to be in Dartmoor at the same time as Frankie Mitchell, a notorious guy in his own right who after been broken out of prison was rumoured to have been executed by the Kray's but this was never proven.

Larry still had escaping on his mind and asked Micky how much longer he had to serve, which was 2 years, he also asked if he knew when the last escape from Dartmoor was. The only escapes had been on the outside working parties not the actual prison. Larry was trying to convince Micky they could make it over the wall from the exercise yard when it was misty and visibility poor, which it often was in Dartmoor at certain times of the year. Larry told him if we can have some hooks made up and obtain rope we could do it. Micky decided he would think about it Larry had nothing to lose he was up for it he would more than likely lose any remission he had at some time or another anyway so why not try and escape. Micky was now warming to the idea and plans were being put in place when Larry was visited in his cell.

"Come on Rushton get your gear together you are being transferred"

"Where?" asked `Larry

"Can't tell you, you will find out when you get there" the officer replied.

Larry was thinking fine anywhere has to be better than here.

Did someone hear about the escape and grass on him or was this transfer scheduled, a question that was maybe answered during his prison transfer, a guard told him there had been rumour of an escape and that's why he was being moved to Exeter a place he would have no chance of escaping from.

In later years Larry was saddened to hear of the death of his buddie Micky Cornwall, also known as "The Laughing Bank Robber" because of his perpetual smile. In September 1975 Micky's dead body, a bullet to the head was found in a shallow grave in Hertfordshire.

CHAPTER 18

EXETER PRISON / ESCAPE

1964

The morning after arriving at Exeter prison, Larry was once again brought before the prison governor who had Larry's prison record in front of him.

"Rushton I can see you have been in a lot of trouble everywhere you have been"

Larry remained silent.

"Mmm yes you have caused a lot of trouble in all the prisons you have been held in. Let me tell you, this is a good prison a secure one and there is no escape from here you can be sure of that, no none has escaped in a long time and we will make sure you don't escape, you will be heavily watched as you have been in previous prisons. Any trouble from you and you will lose some remission. Do you have anything to say?"

"Yes you can keep my remission I have hardly any to lose anyway, you keep it. I don't give a fuck" replied Larry

The governor stared at Larry

"Well you can cut that swearing out"

"Take him away straight to the punishment block and solitary confinement, 14 days"

Whilst in solitary Larry was again assigned to sewing mailbags in his cell but thought no I am not going to do it what is the point. When the officers came to collect the bags and none were done Larry was once again threatened with loss of remission but there was really nothing to lose. After 14 days in solitary Larry was once again brought before the governor where his couldn't care less attitude was questioned along with a warning about future behaviour.

Larry now in a new cell was assessing the prison, most sentences seemed short term so he thought to himself that he probably wouldn't be here for long without being transferred. It was no surprise that Larry had again been assigned to the mailbag workshop, but this one had machines for the real heavy mailbags so there was a bit of both going on. Looking down the workshop Larry noticed an office and observation point above which were old sewing machines and benches piled up to the skylight windows with thin bars on them. This workshop was extremely large and with the seating being set out in rows was also used as a cinema to show films about once a week. As Larry worked away in the workshop he was now plotting another escape something which he mentioned to an inmate he became pals with. As they walked around chatting in the exercise yard they could see the windows on the back of the workshop backed onto a stockyard and beyond that an outside wall. From the exercise yard there was a large gate which led to the stockyard but that wasn't an option as it was too well guarded. Larry's mind was ticking over when suddenly he had it, the best time to escape would be when inmates were watching a film in the mailbag workshop, although many officers would be in attendance Larry saw this as an opportunity.

The finished mailbags were always stacked up by the side of the office, a running jump onto those and it may be possible to climb above the office and then use the old industrial machinery to smash the windows and hopefully knock the bars out. Christmas was coming and that had to be the best time to attempt an escape as this room would host maybe three or four films during the Christmas period.

Larry decided they would attempt the escape whilst a Norman wisdom film was to be shown, this film was to be the last one shown over the Christmas period so it was a case of now or never the opportunity may not come round again. Larry told his fellow inmate to destroy any letters, phone numbers and anything else that would connect him with the outside so that when he was on the run it would be more difficult to track him down. As Larry was on special watch he always had an officer sat close by, either next to him or next but one in the make shift cinema.

The evening arrived, it was Boxing Day, as prisoners from Larry's wing made their way into the cinema to take a seat and as expected an officer was sat right next to Larry. The Norman Wisdom film brought much laughter from the audience including the officers, little did they know what was about to take place. Larry gave the nod to his pal who was sat just a few rows away from Larry with two other inmates who were in on the escape. After giving the nod Larry punched the officer next to him smack on the chin immediately stunning him then all four of them ran down a passage in between the chairs that led to the office where the mailbags were stacked up. Larry was first to reach the mailbags which he jumped onto to access the roof area above the office as did his close pal and the other two inmates. So far so good with all of them now in the roof area the film stopped to a deathly silence. The officers were now in pursuit, Larry armed with a piece of wood he had found warned the officers not to follow or he would take their head off. Whilst Larry was keeping his eye on the officers the other two inmates were throwing machines at the windows and the bars where beginning to bend, they kept bashing away and eventually they broke through. Larry' s close pal was first through the window closely followed by the other two inmates, Larry still watching and taunting the officers was thinking I am going to get left behind here at this rate.

The officers were trying to entice Larry down but that was never going to happen. He just stared back at them

"I have just got one thing to say to you all Merry Christmas!"

and with that he was off and out through the broken window dropping down into the snowy stock yard. The three of them then helped each other to climb over the outside wall before going their separate ways.

Larry now about half a mile away from the prison came across many houses with lights on and thought to himself 'Boxing Day' one of these houses must have some turkey left over. He eventually came across one house where the back door leading to the kitchen was unlocked so let himself in but then noticed a garage to the side of the house which was also unlocked. The garage was full of rubbish loads of boxes and old dust sheets, Larry could hear plenty of activity as the occupants celebrated Christmas and thought no one will come into the garage so it would be a good place to get his head down and lay low. As the celebrating went on Larry was reflecting on the number of Christmas's he had missed and it really got to him as he hid amongst the boxes and rags.

Eventually activities in the house came to an end and all the lights were now out. Larry made his way back to the kitchen to find to his surprise that the door had not been locked. Once in the kitchen he found turkey legs which had not been touched so he took those along with a few mince pies and cake and then hid back in the garage, it was freezing but at least he had some food. Larry considered moving on early morning the following day but decided to stay put for the time being, there was no car in the garage and it was just full of rubbish so the odds of anyone entering the garage was slim. Larry remained in the garage for about twenty four hours then thought the time was right to make a move he put on an old rain coat which he had found amongst all the rubbish then left whilst it was dark.

On foot he came across a college so broke in through a window then searched around for a phone which he found in one of the offices.

Picking up the phone he called Tony a friend of his who lived in London.

"Hi it's me Larry I am out and hoping to make my way over to you"

"Larry you are out, right when you make it to London or close by give me a ring and I will pick you up" replied Tony Larry decided he would stay in the College overnight so with time on his hands he had a good look around and came across some money, not a lot, but at least he had some, he also found some student clothes that he changed into. In the morning he set off walking and reached the outskirts of Exeter where he turned into a lane but as he got about halfway down it he could see police cars in the distance, what should he do now, if he turned around and the police noticed they would be on him like a ton of bricks, there was only one thing to do keep going and front up the situation head on. As Larry was nearing the police they looked at him then waved him on, strangely enough paying close attention to his socks, fortunately Larry had changed out of his prison socks at the college into a pair he had found lying around. That was a close call as he walked away he had no idea where he was but with the help of a few people he spoke to he was now on a coach on his way to London. On arriving in London's Elephant and Castle area he rang Tony who picked him up and took him back to his home.

"Larry you have been all over the news, they have actually managed to capture two of the prisoners that escaped with you"

"Did they give any names?" asked Larry

"They just said they had captured two and you were still on the run. They referred to you as being extremely dangerous and were also keen to capture you because of your previous escape from Leeds"

"Larry don't worry you can stay here as long as you wish"

Larry spent some time at Tony's and some time at Tony's brother's Pete.

"Pete I have been here a few days now it's time to get hold of some money" said Larry

Pete replied

"Larry there are a few things coming up that you might be interested in"

Pete had many connections in and around London and at this particular time was heavily involved in holding up trucks and relieving them of the cargo. Larry as ever was up for it and earned a few quid helping out.

Around this time Larry was thinking about Pat wondering how she was doing but he didn't dare get in touch as he expected the police would be keeping a close eye on her. Larry was now turning his thoughts to Spain again and how good it was so he made contact with a guy he knew who would be able to sort him out with a passport. Whilst waiting for a passport Larry was residing in a flat in the Bayswater area when one morning at about 11 o'clock in the morning there was a knock at his door. The game was up following an underworld tip off the police had tracked him down and he was arrested once again.

The last escapee of the 4 to be re-captured.

Whilst in Police custody he was questioned as to how he had been getting by, they were trying to pin him to some crimes but nothing would stick there was nothing in the flat to tie him into any jobs and the only money he had was what he had in his pocket, the cash for Spain was left with a friend to look after.

Larry spent the evening in a police cell before being transferred the following day to Wandsworth prison yet again. The question going round in his mind was who had grassed on him it wouldn't have been Tony or Pete so who had done so.

On arriving at Wandsworth he was taken straight to the punishment block awaiting transfer back to Exeter Prison.

From Larry's cell he could see prisoners walking around the exercise yard well just the bottom part of their legs and the feet.

One day whilst in his cell a cleaner whispered to him

"Ronnie Biggs sends his best if you need anything just let him know"

Ronnie who spent time with Larry in Lewes Prison must have heard on the grapevine that Larry was down in the punishment block. A couple of days later Ronnie was walking around the exercise yard and when he got to Larry's cell he knelt down and whispered through the small opening

"Larry how long are you going to be down there?"

"I don't know a week maybe two I am to be transferred back to Exeter" replied Larry

Ronnie gave Larry some advice and a possible escape option.

"Do yourself a favour Larry, do your best to try and get yourself out of the punishment block sweet talk them if you have to. I am going to be making one from here before too long"

“I will try my best Ronnie that sounds terrific” replied Larry who was now thinking how he could possibly be moved from his cell.

The next time Larry spoke to the governor he enquired as to how long he was to remain in the punishment block he even suggested he wouldn’t mind serving his time in Wandsworth, but the governor told him there was no chance of that he would have to go back to Exeter to finish his sentence and until he was transferred he would remain where he was. His transfer to Exeter came through a couple of days later and on arriving there he was immediately placed into solitary confinement once again.

A couple of weeks later Ronnie famously escaped, Larry could have been with him if only he could have remained in Wandsworth. If Larry had escaped he would have escaped three times whilst on one sentence, surely that would have been some sort of UK record.

It was now time once again for Larry to be brought before a visiting magistrates who recalled the escape then asked him why he did what he did.

Larry replied with a smile on his face

“You do realise what day it was don’t you”

“Yes we do it was Boxing Day” said the magistrate

“Well there you go wouldn’t you want to go home for Christmas if you were in my position” replied Larry.

Larry continued to swear and hurl abuse at them as he had done many times before and refused to apologise.

He was then taken back to his cell awaiting transfer to another high security prison

CHAPTER 19

PAINTING HIS WAY OUT OF PRISON

1970 – 1974

Larry was never far away from crime and in 1970 he was once again arrested this time his offence was conspiracy to rob. For this offence he was sentenced to 7 years and imprisoned in Hull prison. Whilst inside Hull prison Larry met Paul Sykes a serial offender who made his own rules and lived by them no matter the consequences. Sykes life was peppered with alcohol abuse, petty robberies, and violent crime. Sykes always a fighter did become a professional boxer in 1978 and in 1979 he unsuccessfully challenged John L Gardener for the British and commonwealth titles before his boxing career ended in 1980. Sykes spent over 21 years out of 26 years in 18 prisons up and down the country before he died at the age of 60 in Pinderfields hospital from Cirrhosis of the liver and Pneumonia.

Larry got on well with Sykes but years later it was to have consequences for both of them.

At this time of his life Larry had now had enough of prison life, he had been in and out prison for the last 30 years and this couldn't continue he needed freedom.

Well freedom arrived when he was granted parole in 1974 having served 4 years of his 7 year sentence.

Upon his release Larry once again headed for Blackpool where he moved in with his sister for a while before renting a flat in Lytham St. Annes. Freedom felt so good after spending 20 years or more locked behind bars freedom was something he didn't want taking away from him again. Larry told his family and friends,

"Crime is not on any more I have had enough, 30 years of crime is enough. The time I have spent locked up in prisons has just been a waste of my life"

This was the only time upon his release from a prison that he said "I have had enough"

It was whilst serving his time in Hull prison that Larry began to focus on painting which was without doubt his natural talent, even though he didn't realise so at the time, he was good, very good. The mural he sketched on the prison wall with black wax whilst in Lewes prison should have told him that, the governor even told him how good he was before handing him further solitary confinement for defacing the cell walls. Painting brought a new meaning to Larry's life it was an escape from the boredom of life on the inside and he even gained a scholarship to win a place at a college of art.

His painting and new attitude to life inside without doubt contributed to him earning parole after 4 years of his sentence.

Many of Larry's paintings whilst behind bars where painted with just a shaving brush and toothbrush, but once a month he would be allowed a box of student paints and would paint on anything he could lay his hands on; torn mailbags, pillow cases, sheets, ripped up straight jackets etc. By the time Larry had been released in 1974 he had produced in the region of forty pieces.

CHAPTER 20

A NEW LIFE AWAY FROM CRIME

1974

Larry's life couldn't be more different now he was making a living out of art, most of his paintings and portraits being commissioned works of art. His art took the eye of Rodney Jones the owner of an art gallery in Lytham named "The Quest". Rodney became an agent and good friend of Larry's and in 1976 arranged for Larry's art to be exhibited at an international spring fair in Birmingham alongside many well-known established artists. Larry's paintings were that good they sold out within 10 minutes of opening.

Following the success of the Birmingham spring fair Larry had his first major exhibition in 1977 at Hoylake's John Gerrard gallery. The gallery exhibited his paintings of back streets, clowns, losers and bizarrely one of a scarecrow with a clown's face dressed in a farmer's battle gear, this exhibition was another huge success.

In the same year 1977 Larry flew to America to arrange an exhibition of his art in Washington with a view to clinching an exclusive deal with a leading firm of fine art printers, his style was quite unique and was just what they were looking for to sell prints world-wide, unfortunately this deal never came to fruition.

Moving back to 1974 this was the year that Larry met what was to be his future wife Elaine my sister. Strangely enough it was myself who introduced Larry to Elaine. We were both waiting on serving drinks in the 'Floral Hall' at the seaward end of St. Annes pier. The 'Floral Hall' once a concert / music hall had featured many famous artists in its time, Gracie Fields, Russ Conway and George Formby to name but a few, but at this time in 1974 following a refurbishment the hall represented a Bavarian beer garden and was hosting a seasonal show 'The Tyrolean". One evening Larry and his brother John decided to check the show out and as fate would have it I looked after their table Larry on double vodka with John sticking to the lager, this was a good evening for me as they tipped me handsomely. Just before the show concluded Larry called me over

"Who is that waitress?"

"My sister actually" I replied

Larry quizzed me some more "Would you mind introducing me, I would like to buy her a drink and get yourself one too"

"Will do, cheers"

Elaine had a drink with him but wasn't sure about going out with him so declined the invitation many times.

Larry wasn't going to give up that easily though and after a few more visits to the 'The Tyrolean' finally persuaded Elaine to go out with him.

With Larry now seeing Elaine on a regular basis I was invited along with a friend of mine Alex to do some training with him, weight training followed by rounds on a punch bag. Larry trained most days whilst in prison before his release and it was something he wished to keep up, so he set up a training area within his garage. We would train four or five times a week and he certainly put us through our paces, a session on the weights before three three-minute rounds on the punch bag, believe me three minutes non-stop felt like an eternity. Larry had some strength and power I used to feel sorry for the punch bag you certainly wouldn't want to be on the end of one of his punches.

Larry married Elaine in 1978 and they went on to have two daughters, Melanie in 1978 and Carla in 1982. Now a family it was time to leave the flat / studio behind and move to a more suitable family home, this they did in 1982 when they moved to a detached bungalow with two garages. This property was ideal as Larry was able to convert one of the garages into a new art studio. It was from here that Larry produced his best art and where he lived for the remainder of his life.

Life had never been as good for Larry his work was much sought after and this gave him a real buzz one far greater than the one he got in his darker days, if only he had realised his true potential earlier on in life who knows where it would have led. He was creating a name for himself as a truly talented artist, no sooner was a painting finished it was sold, amongst his cliental was comedian Les Dawson who also resided in Lytham St.Annes.

Larry and Elaine enjoyed a good social life and became well known in the restaurants pubs and clubs in the area, sadly many of them no longer exist or have been taken over.

Amongst their favourites: -

'The Queensway' St.Annes in the days when Frank Conroy managed the place, I remember Frank well, a top bloke, I even had my own wedding reception there.

The 'Town and Country' Blackpool was also a big favourite a top top restaurant. Larry introduced the place to me, I can tell you the beef stroganoff was just one of several amazing dishes on the menu, the best stroganoff I have ever had tasted for sure.

Clubbing wise it was 'The Lemon Tree' Squires Gate, Blackpool, it had everything, floors housing differing types of music, a restaurant and casino, it was the place to be but memberships were like gold dust.

Casino's beside the 'Lemon Tree' the 'Tiberius' in Blackpool and the 'Clifton' in St. Annes were frequently visited. Strangely given Larry's past he was not a big gambler it was just a bit of fun after dining in the establishments. He was certainly not lucky whether it was playing the casino games or poker games at home with the family. I certainly can't remember a time when he had a big win.

Many of the restaurants Larry visited bought oil paintings, and prints from him and it was in one of these restaurants that Larry first met a valuable contact who happened to be in the restaurant one evening and was looking at the oil paintings displayed and being so impressed he asked the restaurant owner who the artist was.

The owner said

"You are in luck, Larry Rushton, he is dining here tonight, I will introduce you."

This person became a very good friend of Larry's and led to Larry's most prestigious commissioned paintings. Larry sitting down in his studio surrounded by his art reflected on his days of crime, the days wasted being locked away in a cell, but as previously mentioned if he had not taken the crooked path his talent as an artist may never have been realised.

For sure he could never have imagined in those dark days what life had in store for him and how his true talent had turned his life around, he was very proud of his achievement.

Larry had certainly lived an eventful life, a crooked path that took 30 years to lead him to whom he became, and yes he finally achieved what he so desired in 1974 to become more widely known as "Larry The Artist" not "Larry The Criminal"

The associated art gallery to this book feature some of Larry's fine art highlighting just how talented and versatile an artist he was. Included in the gallery are some of Larry's most well known paintings.

- The Loser
- Reflections
- Good Day in the City
- Bad Day in the City
- Who wants to be a Millionaire
- Forgotten Village
- Our Street

They say a picture is worth a thousand words, and for Larry the gallery truly does speak for it's self.

The art gallery may be viewed on YouTube by searching with "Larry Rushton Art Gallery."

CHAPTER 21

ONE MORE SENTENCE

Larry and Paul Sykes lives crossed paths once again in 1980 when Larry foolishly agreed to help a business man and friend of his Peter out when his trailer company was heading towards financial ruin due to a union leader organising a series of strikes over pay.

Peter wanted the union strike leader beaten up to avoid more strikes and asked Larry if he knew of anyone that would be up for the job. Larry without really thinking too much about it came up with 'Paul Sykes', this was just about one year since his title fight with John L Gardener so may have been fresh in Larry's mind. Robin, Peter's brother then carried out the contract negotiations.

Sykes assisted by his errand boy Roy carried out the assault for a payment of £1000.

Larry was given £500 for acting as the middleman and approaching Sykes.

With the union leader out of the way for a few months a pay deal with the employees was then agreed.

All five men were eventually arrested and following a court appearance at Preston crown court in December 1980 four were given prison sentences.

Peter 18 months - Larry 12 months - Roy 9 months and Robin 6 months.

Sykes was to be sentenced at a later date as he was facing 4 further charges of assault. In 1981 he was sentenced to 5 years.

An article / Quote by Paul Sykes on Larry

"It was Larry the Brush doing 7 years for conspiracy, who got me going" he admits cheerfully.

"A great artist. Larry even in the nick was getting 10 quid a painting. Last year on the outside he sold one for £11,000 and another one for £18,000"

"He taught me there are beautiful things in life if you are prepared to see, listen and learn. That there are more enjoyable things to read than mucky books and 'Beano'. I owe him a lot"

Also available from Warcry Publishing

Sweet Agony by Paul Sykes

SYKES, Paul; b. 23 May 1946, only son of Walter Sykes and Betty Barlow, market and shop retailers, Wakefield, Yorkshire.

Represented England and County at every amateur boxing level. Contested the British & Commonwealth Heavyweight title as a professional. Holder of Distinction and bar, Royal Life-Saving Society. Qualified football referee. Holder of the British Amateur Weightlifting Record, Deep Knee Bend 5001/2lb.

Much travelled in the UK Prison System: 25 transfers in 20 years to three prison regions, eleven prisons and three special wings.

Educ: Snapethorpe Seconday Modern, Wakefield Technical College. City & Guilds Bricklaying 1966 and 1975. BA (Physical Sciences) Open University (1982).

HIS novel SWEET AGONY won an Arthur Koestler Literary Award in 1988.